The Metaphysics of Knowledge
and Politics in Thomas Aquinas

Other Books of Interest from St. Augustine's Press

James V. Schall, *On the Principles of Taxing Beer:*
And Other Brief Philosophical Essays

James V. Schall, *At a Breezy Time of Day*

Promise Hsu, *China's Quest for Liberty: A Personal History of Freedom*

Marvin R. O'Connell, *Telling Stories that Matter: Memoirs and Essays*

Rémi Brague, *Moderately Modern*

Josef Pieper, *Exercises in the Elements: Essays–Speeches–Notes*

Josef Pieper, *A Journey to Point Omega: Autobiography from 1964*

Josef Pieper, *Traditional Truth, Poetry, Sacrament*

Peter Kreeft, *Ethics for Beginners: 52 "Big Ideas" from 32 Great Minds*

Peter Kreeft, *Socrates' Children: The 100 Greatest Philosophers*

Peter Kreeft, *Summa Philosophica*

Kevin Hart, *Contemplation and Kingdom: Aquinas Reads Richard of St. Victor*

Wayne J. Hankey, *Aquinas's Neoplatonism in the Summa Theologiae on God*

John F. Boyle, *Master Thomas Aquinas and the Fullness of Life*

Robert J. Spitzer, S.J., *Evidence for God from Physics and Philosophy*

Joseph Bottum, *The Decline of the Novel*

D. Q. McInerny, *Being Ethical*

Roger Scruton, *An Intelligent Person's Guide to Modern Culture*

Roger Scruton, *The Meaning of Conservatism: Revised 3rd Edition*

Roger Scruton, *The Politics of Culture and Other Essays*

Roger Scruton, *On Hunting*

Leon J. Podles, *Losing the Good Portion:*
Why Men Are Alienated from Christianity

Allen Mendenhall, *Shouting Softly: Lines on Law, Literature, and Culture*

René Girard, *A Theater of Envy: William Shakespeare*

Marion Montgomery, *With Walker Percy at the Tupperware Party*

The Metaphysics of Knowledge and Politics in Thomas Aquinas

ROCCO BUTTIGLIONE

TRANSLATED BY DANIEL B. GALLAGHER

ST. AUGUSTINE'S PRESS
South Bend, Indiana

Manufactured in the United States of America.

1 2 3 4 5 6   26 25 24 23 22 21 20

Library of Congress Control Number: 2020943143

∞ The paper used in this publication meets the minimum requirements of the American National Standard for Information Sciences – Permanence of Paper for Printed Materials, ANSI Z39.48-1984.

St. Augustine's Press
www.staugustine.net

Introduction

This book presents two studies based on a course I offered at the *Libera Università degli Studi di Urbino* in 1981–1982 entitled "Metaphysics of Knowledge and Politics," as well as a series of lectures I gave at the International Academy of Philosophy in Irving, Texas, in February of 1985.

I owe an enormous debt of gratitude to my students and colleagues, especially Professors Josef Seifert, John Crosby, and Michael Healey, who, through lively discussions helped me to make notable improvements to the work.

In a certain sense, these two studies are part of a larger attempt to go beyond the notion "modern" as it pertains to philosophy. There is a tendency to view the relationship between the ancient/Christian philosophy of being and the modern philosophy of consciousness and becoming as oppositional. Such a tendency forces us to choose between classical and modern thought as if it were merely a choice between being and becoming. It does little to help us solve the false problem of the "modern" in philosophy. It rests on an implicit assumption that the human being has changed so radically in the course of history that we are unable to distinguish between different philosophical schools on the basis of their emphases, but only on the basis of their fundamental structures. This entails not a difference in how problems are solved but in how they are formulated.

Although the idea that the human person can change completely in the course of history accords perfectly with categories of modern thought, it is challenged by the authentic philosophy of being. Such a philosophy cannot allow the fundamental ontic-metaphysical structure of "man" as a being *(ens)* to change over time. When the problem of how to oppose the "modern" in philosophy—a problem that concerns many scholars of the classical tradition—is approached in this way, it is transformed into the problem of how to overcome the category of the "modern" so as to recover philosophy's essential unity.

This is the direction in which some phenomenologists are moving today, and in particular the realist phenomenology arising out of Munich, whose principal representative is Josef Seifert.[1]

Although beginning with significantly different presuppositions, this is the same direction taken by the philosophy (which is really a history of philosophy) cultivated by Augusto Del Noce, who perhaps best understood the crisis of the Italian historical tradition and who made a groundbreaking attempt to recover the philosophy of being.[2] His work, like my previous work, is characterized by a complex vision of the history of philosophy. The critical recovery of the philosophy of being, so necessary today, must begin, in a certain sense, from the world of the human and the sphere of the subject, a particular emphasis in the philosophy of consciousness. It is necessary to recover "being" by beginning with human experience as being's necessary implication, and therefore by beginning with an understanding of individual and historical affairs. Ontic-metaphysical categories are an indispensable key for understanding these affairs.

This is why political philosophy is so important. The modern philosophy of consciousness goes beyond political action to investigate how the individual overcomes solipsism. But does it do this with due respect for the *immanent* laws of political action? Politics is where the balance between the universal and the particular is best put to the test, earmarking it with a philosophical position. From this point of view, political philosophy is not simply "secondary" among other kinds of philosophy, rather the very locus where the entire coherence of a philosophical position is put to the test. It therefore constitutes the apex of a philosophical position.

The studies contained in this book strive to reconstruct points of correspondence and linkages between Thomas Aquinas's political philosophy and his anthropology and metaphysics of knowledge. The guiding hypothesis is that the philosophy of Aristotle can still be of tremendous help in understanding a large part of modern philosophy, and that the medieval contention that Aristotle was the philosopher *par excellence* still contains a good bit of truth insofar as subsequent philosophy can be considered a continuous development of various aspects of his thought.

---

1   Josef Seifert, *Verso una fondazione fenomenologica della metafisica classica* (Milano: Vita e Pensiero, 1986).

2   Augusto Del Noce, *Il problema dell'ateismo* (Bologna: Il Mulino, 1970).

Modern genetic-critical research has identified three layers of Aristotle's thought even if scholars are not in agreement about how they are interrelated.[3] We can distinguish between (1) the Platonized Aristotle who reconsiders the Platonic doctrine of ideas and uses it to build his own doctrine of separate substances, (2) the realist Aristotle who opposes Platonic metaphysics with his own metaphysics, and (3) Aristotle the empiricist and naturalist who eventually leaves behind metaphysical problems *per se*.

The discovery of various levels in Aristotle's work has opened the door to an array of interpretations regarding not only his thought but, in a more basic way, the criteria used by Andronicus of Rhodes to come up with an edition of Aristotle's works: the edition scholars use today to understand Aristotle's *corpus*. Moraux, however, has rightly noted a tendency toward empirical research in Aristotle's work, a tendency that emerges if we look closely at the final years of the Academy. We only need to recall Plato's *Timeaus*.[4]

On the other hand, Aristotle, even while he still considered himself a member of the Academy, never adhered to Plato's notion of separate ideas as expounded in the *Phaedrus* or the *Republic*. That notion was already in crisis in the final phase of Plato's career as evident in the *Parmenides*. Indeed, Aristotle's entire thought is based on the crisis of Platonism. It is quite probable, Moraux continues, that Aristotle saw no contradiction in the simultaneous emphasis on separate substance and sensible reality. In other words, it is safe to say that his thought was continually evolving, albeit not in a linear manner. He was constantly adjusting rather than rejecting what had preceded him.

3   At the beginning of this movement we find the fundamental work of Werner Jaeger in *Aristoteles: Grundlegung einer Geschichte seiner Entwicklung* (Berlin: Widemann, 1923). Similar in method but with different results is Paul Gohlke. See his complex work *Aristoteles und sein Werk* (Paderborn: Schöningh, 1948) and *Die Entstehung der aristotelischen Prinzipienlehre* (Tübingen: Mohr, 1954). For a critical, balanced, and still current treatment, see Giovanni Reale, *Introduzione a Aristotele* (Roma-Bari: Laterza, 1982). By the same author, see also *Il concetto di filosofia prima e l'unità della metafisica di Aristotele* (Milano: Vita e Pensiero, 1967), and by Enrico Berti, see *Aristotele: dalla dialettica all filosofia prima* (Padova: CEDAM, 1977).

4   Paul Moraux, *Aristote et Saint Thomas d'Aquin* (Nauwelaerts-Louvain-Paris: Publicatiòns universitaires de Louvain/Editions Beatrice, 1957).

Despite its inability to yield a complete reconstruction of Aristotle's thought, the genetic-critical school still has its merit. It has forced us to look at Aristotle through a new lens. It has helped us to understand not only that he had no fear of asking questions and reconsidering previous doctrines that did not conform with new insights and new evidence, but also that his works can be read from several different angles. It is precisely these insights of modern Aristotelian scholarship that give plausibility to the idea that philosophy developed as a systematic interpretation of the Stagirite, such that Aristotle became the standard for further philosophical discussion.

A similar criterion could be applied to our reading of medieval philosophy. It is not difficult to see medieval philosophy as a moderate Aristotelianism that opts for a Platonized interpretation and therefore favors the Aristotelian texts reflecting this spirit. Both the naturalistic and somewhat heterodox Aristotelianism, as well as the "standard" Aristotelianism represented by Aquinas, strive for a sort of unity and therefore develop Aristotle beyond his original limits to achieve this result. In his *Avicenna und die aristotelische Linke,* Bloch gives us a sketch of the opposition between the Aristotelian right and the Aristotelian left.

It would seem preferable and more in conformity with the factual data to view the philosophical controversy of the second half of the thirteenth century as a triptych in the following way. On the right we have an eclectic and neo-Platonized Aristotelianism as found in William of Saint-Amour, Gérard D'Abbeville, Stephen Tempier, John Peckham, Matteo d'Acquasparta, and others. On the left we have the heterodox Aristotelianism of Siger of Brabant. In the center we have Aquinas accompanied by Pietro di Tarantasia, Peter of Auvergne, and James of Douai. The triptych at the University of Paris seems to correspond to the modern commentators' tripartite reading of Aristotle except for the fact that the naturalistic right (as Aquinas would show in his polemic against it) is deeply affected by neo-Platonism. Furthermore, while pure naturalistic Aristotelianism would correspond to a modern form of empiricism, heterodox Aristotelianism would move in a direction toward modern idealism and dialectical materialism.

Aquinas's intention is different. He wants to save the Aristotelian framework from splintering into various competing schools by reassembling the original framework in a way that will keep the balance between empirical individuality and ideal universality. To Aquinas, it seems that this equilibrium is the most adequate philosophical expression of the Christian conception of God's personhood and the essential personhood of human beings.

*

In political philosophy, the problem of equilibrium between the particular and the universal is the problem of a citizen's liberty and his or her relation to the state. In Aristotle's political theory, there are elements that both affirm and deny the right of an individual subject with respect to the political community. How this plays out depends more generally on Aristotle's anthropological vision and his metaphysics of knowledge. If the individual subject does nothing more than support an overarching knowing process that is eminently collective and whose subject is the species as a whole, it will be difficult to see a need to safeguard the rights of the individual within the political community. If the individual person is not the subject of knowledge, neither can he or she be a subject of responsibility and action nor a subject enjoying certain rights.

The solutions Aquinas gives to the problems of political liberty and knowledge are marvelously coherent and mutually supportive. These solutions, when read reciprocally, constitute an *ad litteram* critique of the modern tendency toward totalitarianism both in an anthropological sense and in political theory and practice.

Part I
Observations on Aquinas's Commentary on Aristotle's *Politics*: The Problem of Subjectivity and Totality

Introduction

Scholars of Aquinas's political philosophy generally do not make much use of his commentary on Aristotle's *Politics*. The reason for this benign neglect is not difficult to ascertain: Aquinas's text is essentially an exact paraphrase of Aristotle, making it difficult to tease out the commentator's own original thought.[5] An initial reading evokes a certain admiration for Aquinas's

---

5   Moreover, unlike other medieval authors, it does not seem that Aquinas uses other Aristotelian commentaries as a fixed reference point for his own work. On Aquinas as a commentator on Aristotle, see Georges Ducoin, "*Saint Thomas commentateur d'Aristote. Etude sur le commentaire thomiste du livre des Metaphysiques d'Aristote*," *Archives de Philosophie*, 20 (1957), pp. 392–445; Gérard Verbeke, *Themistius. Commentaire sur le traité l'utilisation du Commentaire dans l'oeuvre de Saint Thomas d'Aquin* (Louvain: Publications universitaires de Louvain, 1957); Rhabanus Laubenthal, *Das Verhältnis des heiligen Thomas von Aquin zu den Arabern in sienem Physikkommentar* (Kallmünz: M. Lasaleben, 1934); Jean Isaac, O. P., *Le peri Hermeneias en Occident de Boèce à saint Thomas* (Paris: Vrin, 1953); Gérard Verbeke, "*Ammonius et Saint Thomas. Deux commentaires sur le Peri Hermeneis de Aritote*," *Revue Philosophique de Louvain*, 54 (1956), pp. 228–253. In regard to the text that interests us here, Conor Martin has ruled out the possibility that Aquinas's commentary is dependent on Albert the Great's, and simultaneously holds that it is impossible to prove a definite dependency upon, or at least a relation to, other commentaries. See *The Commentaries on the Politics of Aristotle in the late Thirteenth and early Fourteenth Century, with reference to the Thought and Political Life of the Time*, Ph.D. Thesis (Oxford, 1949).

exegetical skills, but such a reading also leaves us thoroughly convinced that we are dealing with a scholastic, pedagogical work, the basic aim of which is to teach others what Aristotle thought.

Those familiar with the Stagirite's text know well how his style tends to be convoluted, fragmented, and terse. It is neither easy to comprehend nor to render into a smooth translation. This challenge, with which even a contemporary commentator on Aristotle must contend, was even more acute in the Middle Ages due to the nature and quality of the translations available at the time. More often than not, one only had access to a retranslation of a translation and therefore had to confront all the problems such remote distance from the original text entails. Moreover, the art of translation was still in its initial stages of development.[6] Consequently, ascertaining the meaning of Aristotle's text was an arduous task in the Middle Ages. A good commentator was absolutely crucial. The authority and skill of the commentator were serious considerations for readers who depended so heavily on the quality of his work.

Against this background, we can readily understand and appreciate the significance of Aquinas's commentaries. On the one hand, he went to great lengths to obtain accurate translations of the original texts. This is why he elicited the help of William of Moerbeke, whose knowledge of Greek was extraordinary. Aquinas placed complete trust in William to produce direct translations of Aristotle's most important works.[7] William worked according to an "even loan" or "exact exchange" model of translation (*de verbo ad verbum* according to Henry of Hervodia). Striving for strict fidelity to the literal meaning of the original text, he worked with such precision that there is hardly ever a doubt concerning the exact Greek

---

6   See Martin Grabmann, "Forschungen über die lateinischen Aristoteles Übersetzungen des XIII Jahrhunderts," *Beiträge zur Geschichte der Philosophie des Mittelalters* (Münster: Aschendorff, 1917); D. J. Allan, "Mediaeval Versions of Aristotle's De Caelo on the commentary of Simplicius," *Mediaeval and Renaissance Studies,* 2 (1950), pp. 82–120; Franze Pelster, "Die Übersetzungen der aristotelischen Metaphysik in den Werken des hl. Thomas von Aquin," *Gregorianum,* 16 (1935), pp. 325–348 and 531–561, and *Gregorianum,* 17 (1936), pp. 377–406.

7   See Martin Grabmann, *Guglielmo di Moerbeke, O. P., Il traduttore delle opere di Aristotele* (Rome: Pontificia Università Gregoriana, 1946).

word corresponding to each and every Latin term.[8] This choice of literality has enabled modern scholars of Aristotle's *Politics* to reconstruct the original text William must have used when rendering the Latin version.[9] Even though it guaranteed a reliable version of Aristotle's text, the use of this methodology also made reading the translated version extremely difficult for anyone lacking the adequate hermeneutical preparation. The text, in effect, is often obscure and confusing. Thus the primary task of the commentator is to produce an integrated lexicographical aid that matches the content of the original work to the capacities of the average reader. His goal is not necessarily to summarize the original content and expound on it through his own philosophical interpretation; he rather aims to paraphrase it.

These considerations not only give us a greater appreciation for the importance of this type of work, but also help us to understand why the commentary often shows little interest in original philosophical speculation. Even though it gives us a better insight into the Stagirite's thought, we learn little about Aquinas's own philosophical vision through these texts.

A closer look shows us another thorny issue in interpreting Aquinas's commentaries. A commentator is necessary not only because of the obscurity of the original text and the difficulties Latin readers have in grasping the concepts of Greek philosophy, but also because of the risk of heresy. In the Middle Ages, Aristotle was often regarded as the provoker of heterodox

8   See Franz Susemihl, *Aristotelis Politicorum Libri Octo cum vetusta translatione Guillermi de Moerbeka* (Leipzig: Teubner, 1872) and also *Aristoteles Latinus XXIX.i: Politica (Libri I–II. 11). Translatio prior imperfecta interprete Guillermo de Moerbeka*, ed. Petrus Michaud-Quentin (Paris: Desclée de Brouwer, 1961). On the use of the *Politics,* see I. T. Eschmann, O. P., "The Quotations of Aristotle's Politics in St. Thomas's *Lectura super Mattheum*," *Mediaeval Studies,* 18 (1956), pp. 232–240. In the *Summa Theologiae* there are frequent citations of the first two books, less from the third, and very few from the last sections. Aquinas's *Commentary* stops at Book III, Chapter 6. The work was subsequently completed by Peter of Auvergne.

9   W. D. Ross, taking into consideration the opinions of Franz Susemihl and Otto Immisch, includes William of Moerbeke's translation among the other *codices* that form the basis of his own edition of the *Politics;* he cites Moerbeke's version as codex Γ. See *Aristotelis Politica: Recognovit brevique adnotatione critica instruxit*, W. D. Ross (Oxford: Oxford University Press, (1957).

ideas.[10] The commentator therefore had the additional task of assuring a "safe" translation purged of anti-Christian elements, or at least those elements susceptible to an anti-Christian interpretation.

The need for vigilance was particularly strong during the years when Aquinas was composing his commentaries. The University of Paris was the seat of a thriving philosophical school that purported a decidedly naturalistic reading of the Stagirite.[11] To interpret Aristotle in such a tense environment was hardly a neutral or inconsequential task.

Broadly speaking, Aquinas's interpretive method involves a three-step process: The first step is to facilitate a smooth reading of Aristotle's text; the second step aims at a systematic understanding of the original author's intent precisely by drawing attention to difficult passages by means of an in-depth comparison with other *loci* and the original author's general principles. The goal is to penetrate Aristotle's *intentio profundior* and, in a certain sense, to correct him on the basis of his own principles. The third phase aims to understand not only "*quid Aristoteles senserit*" but "*quomodo se habeat veritas rerum.*" This is the level at which Aquinas begins to introduce his own thought as he moves from a simple

10   The first condemnation was issued in 1210 at the Council of the ecclesiastical province of Sens, pronounced by Peter de Corbeil, Archbishop of Paris. The teaching of *libri Aristotelis de naturali philosophia* was prohibited. In 1215, Cardinal Robert di Courçon extended the prohibition to the *libri de metaphysica*. The teaching of Aristotelian logic, however, remained licit, as it had already become commonplace in the preceding century. In a letter addressed to professors and students of the University of Paris, dated April 13th, 1231, Pope Gregory IX reaffirms the prohibition against Aristotelian teaching, but only *ad tempus* until the texts were examined and emended. The interdict was reissued in 1245 (this time extending also to the University of Toulouse), and again in 1263 until the great condemnation of 1277, which involved, even if only marginally, Aquinas himself. We should note, however, that these interdicts were local: Parisian, or French at most. Beyond that—for example at Oxford—the teaching of Aristotle continued undisturbed until the beginning of the next century.

11   See E. H. Weber, *La controverse de 1270 à l'Université de Paris et son retentissement sur la pensée de S. Thomas d'Aquin* (Paris: Vrin, 1970) and Fernand Van Steenberghen, *Maître Siger de Brabant* (Louvain-Paris: Publications universitaires, 1977).

exposition to a philosophical interpretation that goes beyond the original text.

Unfortunately, the text of his commentary on the *Politics* offers us few examples of the second and third phases, except perhaps in the Prologue. Otherwise he limits himself to an extremely faithful explanation of the literal meaning of the text. Therefore, an interpreter interested in the philosophical meaning of the text faces a choice: One must either assert a complete identification of Aquinas's thought with Aristotle's, or discard the *Commentary on the Politics* since it is of no use in reconstructing Aquinas's original thought.

In reality, the situation is not so simple. On the one hand, the commentary on Aristotle's *Politics* is a particularly rich text for gaining an exact understanding of Aquinas's political thought precisely *because* of the difficulty alluded to above. Indeed, that difficulty forces us to take into account the fundamental problem of the nature and extent of any connection between Aristotle's thought and Aquinas's. There is little doubt that Aquinas did not consciously set out to construct a philosophy separate from Aristotle's. But it is equally doubtful that Aquinas's philosophical originality consists in, or has methodological roots in, an effort to construe an interpretation of Aristotle's text compatible with Christian dogma each and every time a potential contradiction arises. Thus it is true that in Aquinas's commentary we are dealing not with purely original thought but some level of interpretation. Yet the result is an *orientated interpretation;* in other words it is a systematic—as opposed to an occasional—variation of the original text. We could say that we are face-to-face with *an original thought which is developed through a direct, on-going encounter with the Stagirite* by means of a hermeneutical approach that opens up surprisingly fresh and original vistas—vistas that may not contradict the author's original intent but are not explicitly indicated by him.

The subject of the *Politics* unfolds in such a way that it seems to relate to the tenets of Christianity only tenuously. This would explain why Aquinas limits himself to a literal exposition with no particular attempt to reinterpret or correct the original. In any case, the text is particularly important for us today since so few Thomistic works deal directly and explicitly with social and political philosophy. Moreover, among the few texts that are available to us, the Commentary on the *Politics* is perhaps the most wide-ranging. Our reading of the text will be guided by a desire to discover keys for translating Aristotelian politics into Thomistic politics; in other words, if we seek to identify the appropriate viewpoint from which—as in other areas of Aquinas's philosophy—we can perceive where his conceptual framework and his modifications of important concepts (which initially seem to be simply a matter of emphasis) either evolve or remain essentially unchanged in comparison with Aristotle's original text. In this way, all of Aristotle's politics will be useful, but we will have to organize that content around a fundamentally new center of gravity.

We will try to identify that new center of gravity by analyzing the methodological guidelines given in the *Proemium* that will assist us in recognizing the significant differences between Aristotle's text and Aquinas's paraphrase of it. In fact, whenever possible, Aquinas prefers not to correct Aristotle openly but to furnish his own version in order to sharpen and clarify the Stagirite's thought. We will then try to integrate our survey of the salient differences with other parts of the Thomistic corpus that essentially deal with the same theme.

I should add right away that the main point of disparity between Aristotle's text and Aquinas's commentary revolves around the problem of how the individual relates to the "whole"; that is, the problem of the effective "absorption" of the individual into the political community. This problem particularly comes into play in the philosophical discussion of slavery. In fact, the slave is *par excellence* someone who does not transcend the social dimension but remains completely enwrapped in it. Not only does he lack an end above and beyond the city-state, he also lacks the capacity to transcend the order of the family insofar as his entire purpose within the family unit is to be possessed as a *res*. Consequently, it is precisely by looking at Aquinas's attitude toward the question of slavery that an avenue opens up for a possible reconstruction of Aristotle's politics from a uniquely Thomistic point of view.[12]

---

12 This is particularly interesting in the contemporary setting where the great philosophical controversies seem to have shifted from the fields of metaphysics and gnoseology to politics and social philosophy.

1. The methodology outlined in the Proemium

In the *Proemium* of the *Commentary on Aristotle's Politics*, Aquinas lists some of the basic metaphysical principles that guide our understanding of political phenomena, situate politics within the wider range of human activities, and place the philosophical science of politics within the wider context of philosophical wisdom. As we will have occasion to see later on, the *Proemium* is extremely important from a methodological point of view; in fact, it sketches the most fundamental issue driving political theory throughout its long and tortuous history—namely, how does the individual relate to the whole, and what specific characteristics of each allow us to draw connections between the two?

First of all, Aquinas recalls the axiom *"art imitates nature."*[13] The word "nature" here designates the entire range of objects and phenomena we discover as already *given* in the world and which constitute the unshakeable starting point for all human action. By the word "art" we mean those things wrought by human power. In other words, the transformation of natural realities by human action guided by a rational rule (*recta ratio*). Nature furnishes the irreducible *primary matter* upon which human activity is carried out. Man cannot create something out of nothing. Human creation is always a "secondary creation" in that it collaborates with God's creative activity of imparting forms to the things of this world, thus transforming them from *objects in the natural world* to *objects in the human world*. Nature does not simply furnish the acting subject with raw material for his or her artistic use or some object for further development; rather, nature gives art its fundamental *modus operandi*. Human creation imitates divine creation in the same way that works of art imitate "works of nature."

The relationship between works of art and works of nature is in turn regulated by the relationship between their respective principles. The basic principle for works of nature is the divine intellect; the principle for works of art is the human intellect. This "derives from the divine intellect according to a certain similitude."[14] The similarity between the human intellect and the divine intellect (which is the basis for the human person as *imago Dei*)

13   *In Octo Libros Politicorum Aristotelis Expositio*, n. 1.
14   *Ibid.*

is the reference point for the relation between works of art and works of nature. A human person must examine works of nature before he or she can successfully model his or her own creative potential after the creative power of God. The art (i.e., "work") through which human beings modify nature is therefore situated within a dialogue between human and divine intellects. By discovering traces of the divine intellect (through which human artistic efforts can be classified as "work") in natural objects, human beings learn to master and exercise their own creative powers. Man, Aquinas writes, is like an apprentice standing at his master's side, carefully observing the way the master works so that by imitating him he learns to work in the same way. Such a comparison shows Aquinas's high esteem for human work and its inherent dignity. In his labor, man *resembles God*. This resemblance, however, is a *relative resemblance*—or more precisely an *analogy*—that in no way eliminates the more radical *qualitative difference*. If the human person were able to imitate divine "work" in such a way that he could *reproduce* or *recreate* the objects of nature, he would effectively become *another God*. This is precisely the illusion of any Promethean philosophy that claims man can negate the given world and construct another one in its place—a world entirely of his own making. Of course, from this viewpoint the status of philosophical thought also changes. Instead of dividing philosophy into *speculative* knowledge, which reflects the work of nature, and *practical* knowledge, which guides the action of human work, philosophy is completely transformed into a *philosophy of praxis*.[15] From the Promethean point of view even nature, insofar as it is entirely *re-created* by man, can be considered a work of art and is therefore subject to the normal rules of all the arts.

Conversely, Aquinas insists on a fundamental distinction between art and nature. Nature offers the artist the material for his or her action as well as the pattern for his or her mode of operation; furthermore, artists can turn to the material realm to understand the work of nature and, within certain limits, their own way of working. But they cannot bring about what is proper to nature alone.[16] This is precisely the basis for the distinction

---

15   Not only historical/dialectical materialism, but also—though with a different thrust—German idealism might be considered the result of eliminating the qualitative difference between *ars* and *natura*.

16   Cf. Stefan Wyszyński, *Duch Pracy Ludzkiej* (Włocławek: 1946).

between the speculative sciences and the practical sciences. Whereas the speculative sciences (which regard natural things) pertain only to knowledge, the practical sciences pertain both to knowledge and to operation. In the practical sciences, we not only *know* the external world of nature and our interior nature, we also *perform* our actions on this epistemological basis. In other words, in acting, we allow ourselves to be guided by nature.[17]

In a certain sense, we can say that we possess an "external" knowledge of natural things, but we do not know *the principle of their creation*. When it comes to works of art, that is, the things we make, we also know their principle of creation. For this reason, it would not be incorrect to call ourselves creators—but *not in the same way as God* even though *we are similar to God*.

Nature begins with the simple before moving on to the complex.[18] The individual elements of nature are part of an overall project that links them to one other in such a way that they become integrated into a larger whole. The whole is the end toward which all the parts tend; hence, the parts can be understood adequately only insofar they relate to the whole. Proceeding in a manner according to the imitation of nature, art also moves from the simple to the complex. The totality is a state of perfection in which the parts can truly be themselves, each carrying out its proper function. Finally, human knowledge also proceeds from the simple to the complex (i.e., the composite).

We must, however, be careful in applying this principle, not only with respect to the objects we produce and judge by our faculty of reason, but also with respect to ourselves and the "forms" we impart to things using our faculty of reason whenever we enter into relationships with others.[19] The whole toward which individual human beings are ordered is the human community. The human community is composed of different kinds of sub-communities variously interlinked with one another, but it is ultimately the city-state *(polis)* that is the perfect human community, encompassing all the others and within which are contained the elements necessary to live well. Because artifacts are ordered to us and our ultimate end, the *polis* is

---

17 *In Octo Libros Politicorum Aristotelis Expositio,* n. 2.
18 *Ibid.,* n. 3.
19 *Ibid.,* n. 4.

the most important reference point for every subordinate "whole" known by human reason.

From what we have said thus far, Aquinas draws three important conclusions: First, a (philosophical) science of politics is not only legitimate but necessary. The totality—which we call the *polis*—is not impervious to rational judgment. Human reason is able to comprehend it and make it an object of philosophical reflection. Aquinas thus demonstrates that he is thoroughly convinced of the *rationality* of politics.[20]

Secondly, Aquinas affirms that political philosophy is a practical philosophy. Reason does not limit itself to knowing the city-state; it also knows that the city-state is a *human* work and therefore must be directed by the light of reason. Political action involves human responsibility, and political philosophy is an indispensable aid to carrying out this responsibility. Moreover, political philosophy is *a moral science*. Aquinas, remaining faithful to Aristotle's classification, divides the practical sciences into mechanical and moral sciences. This division stems from the idea of a twofold effect of human action. There are actions that are simply directed toward a modification of the external environment upon which man exercises his power. This type of action passes from the subject to the object in which it terminates and reaches a state of rest. Thus, when a blacksmith molds a tool by bending the iron, the effect of his action (at least on the surface) is simply the production of a determined instrument. However, there are also actions that do not pass over into the object but remain within the subject: Choosing and willing, for example, involve a modification not of the object but of the acting subject. Even if they are the basis for subsequent action that modifies reality, intransitive actions are first and foremost modifications of the subject who performs them. By becoming good through the performance of good actions or bad through the performance of bad actions, we transform ourselves in addition to conferring a moral quality on the external actions we perform. Actions that pass over from the subject to an object are studied by the mechanical sciences, while those that remain within the subject are studied by the moral sciences.[21]

20   *Ibid.*, n. 5.
21   *Ibid.*, n. 6.

Thirdly, Aquinas delineates the relationship between political philosophy and the other practical sciences. Political philosophy stands at the point of convergence and synthesis of all practical knowledge.[22] The mechanical sciences have the human person as their ultimate end; they work together for the building and administration of the just city-state, but it is ultimately political philosophy that manifests their proper place and function within civil society. In fact, even if the human person is his own end, the immediate object of the mechanical sciences is not man *qua* man, but the adequate completion of this or that human task. It is precisely for this reason that political philosophy is the apex of practical philosophy insofar as it is primarily concerned with human affairs.

Fourthly, Aquinas describes the proper methodology of political philosophy. This philosophy, in a way similar to speculative inquiry, begins with a consideration of the individual parts of the *polis* and then proceeds to show how they interact among themselves within a totality directed toward a specific end. Moreover, political philosophy shows how it is possible for an individual person to perform actions that simultaneously pertain to his own good and to the life of the city-state in a way that conforms to the practical nature of each.[23]

2. Two problems: *ars et totum*

After this brief summary of the Prologue, it would be worth pausing to reflect on two important hermeneutical questions. The first can be formulated in this way: How exactly should we translate the word *ars*? The term covers a whole range of meanings from "art" to "labor." Art (in the sense of the "fine arts") is *par excellence* a creative human activity that imitates God's creative work. There is no doubt that for Thomas *ars* also means the fabrication of objects for common use and a kind of intelligent modification of nature through human effort.

At the same time, "work" is not entirely satisfactory translation. In Aquinas, *ars* has the quality of a spirituality or intelligence in the human quest to master the material realm. But this does not exactly correspond

22 *Ibid.*, n. 7.
23 *Ibid.*, n. 8.

with what Aquinas means by human work—especially servile work—later in the Commentary. With respect to its basic underlying principle, *ars*—a type of intelligence—draws us into a similarity with God that is the apex of human dignity. Can we say the same thing about work in general?

The question must remain open. A definitive interpretation of Aquinas's entire thought, however, will depend heavily on how we answer this question.[24] It is not likely that we will find an unambiguous response buried in the text since it is primarily a commentary on Aristotle. In other words, the text as we have it is a *commentary on another author's thought* in which Aquinas, given his undeniable admiration for the Stagirite's philosophy, does not feel free to reveal completely his own thinking. Therefore, if we want to examine this point more deeply, we will have to compare the Commentary on Aristotle's *Politics* with other passages in Aquinas's writings.

The second hermeneutical problem involves the "whole." The term used by Thomas is *totum*. Simply translating it as "totality" already interjects an interpretation. "Totality" is a technical term employed by Hegelian philosophy. Even though some authors try to use it outside that tradition, it inevitably retains the shades of meaning it acquired within its original Hegelian context. In one sense it points to a teleological connection between various parts: The whole is not only the sum of the parts but their interconnectedness in view of a meaning that goes above and beyond the individual parts taken collectively. In Hegel's understanding of the "whole," the "part" is taken away, transcended but simultaneously preserved. For Hegel, *the whole is more real and incomparably more valuable than the parts.* This has obvious implications for the relationship between the *polis* and the individual citizen.

To a certain extent Hegel's view is a continuation and interpretation of Aristotle's original treatment of the problem. In fact, there is an unbroken line of thought that runs from medieval Aristotelianism to Hegel. It is a line of thought that has been meticulously studied by Ernst Bloch in his

---

24 If we take *ars* strictly in the sense of "work," we can easily detect a modern theology of work in Aquinas as delineated in the encyclical *Laborem Exercens*. But this would be somewhat of a stretch, as we will see shortly.

Avicenna und die aristotelishe Linke,[25] and Galvano Della Volpe in *Hegel romantico e mistico.*[26] The line starts with a heterodox and naturalistic Aristotelianism and branches off into Meister Eckhart, on the one hand, and Giordano Bruno, on the other.

Naturally, the Christian conviction that the greatest good of the individual human person is the salvation of his or her soul stands in direct opposition to the notion that the citizen is inescapably absorbed by the political community. Since man has the internal capacity to bring about an encounter with the divine Absolute, he contains within himself, so to speak, a dignity superior to that of the entire human race of which the *polis* is but an articulation (given that, according to this view, the human species is taken in a purely naturalistic sense).

It seems that a satisfactory answer to this problem depends on a careful and precise interpretation of two particular passages in the Prologue. The first reads:

> *Et quia ea quae in usum hominis veniunt ordinantur ad hominem sicut ad finem, qui est principalior his quae sunt ad finem, ideo necesse est quod hoc totum quod est civitas sit principalius omnibus totis, quae ratione humana cognosci et constitui possunt.*[27]

The problem is this: What exactly does it mean to say that "the whole which is the city-state" is "more important that all the totalities that can be known and constituted by human reason"? More specifically, is man to be included among those totalities? If we respond negatively, we risk accepting an anarchical position that jeopardizes the foundation of legitimate political power. If we respond positively, we risk legitimizing the absolutization of that power and dissolving man and his rights into a totalitarian entity of a higher order, be it the "state," "race," or "social class."

25 Ernst Bloch, *Avicenna und die aristotelishe Linke* (Berlin: Suhrkamp Verlag, 1963).

26 Galvano Della Volpe, *Hegel romantico e mistico* (Florence: Le Monnier, 1929).

27 *In Octo Libros Politicorum Aristotelis Expositio,* n. 4. "Since the things man seeks to make use of are ordered to man as their end—who is more important than the things ordered to that end—it is just as necessary for the 'whole' of the city-state to be the most important whole among all 'wholes' known and constituted by man."

In all likelihood, the most reasonable response would be to say that in the first part of the passage quoted above, man himself is not included among the totalities inserted into the *polis* in a subordinate way, and that the second part articulates a second term to set up a comparison.

In fact, Aquinas says that "since all the things man finds himself using are ordered to him as their end, and the end is more important that the things that serve that end, therefore [...]."[28] Thus there is a parallelism between man and the city-state on the one hand, and the things that serve his end and "all the totalities that can be known and constituted by human reason" on the other. It therefore seems that those totalities should be understood as forms of activity (i.e., arts) that rationally arrange the various things that serve him in an instrumental way. The city-state is elevated to the level of "end" by its resemblance to man, but how the relationship between the two ends is not entirely clear. We can think, for example, that in reality the city-state is not, so to speak, something "other" than man ("man" understood from the viewpoint of self-expansion through interpersonal relation), such that *man* is considered from the viewpoint of his action and inter-subjectivity. This seems to be a legitimate reading of the passage, but it is already an attempt to integrate the text rather than a simple explanation of it. The relationship between man understood as empirical subjectivity and "man" as the city-state will still have to be explained, as it is by Socrates's method in the *Republic*.[29]

The complexity of the question is further evident in the fact that even though an immediate interpretation of the above-cited text forces us to rule out the possibility of a complete subordination of the human being to the city-state, a bit earlier we read that man is one of the "wholes" subordinated to reason. Aquinas writes:

> *Cum autem ratio humana disponere habeat non solum de his quae in usum hominis veniunt, sed etiam de ipsis hominibus qui ratione*

28   *Ibid.*
29   Bk. 2, chap. 9e.

reguntur [...] multos homines ordinat in unam quamdam communi-
tatem.[30]

Here the idea of the individual's complete subordination to the community is much sharper and clearer, even if it receives definitive confirmation only if the *ratio* regulating the relationship between the individual and the community is conceived as falling entirely on the side of the community.

The second text of Aquinas regarding the totality occurs three paragraphs earlier:

> *Procedit autem natura in sua operatione ex simplicibus ad composita;*
> *ita quod in eis quae per operationem naturae fiunt, quod est maxime*
> *compositum est perfectum et totum et finis aliorum, sicut apparet in*
> *omnibus totis respectu suarum partium. Unde et ratio hominis*
> *operativa ex simplicibus ad composita procedit tamquam ex imperfectis*
> *ad perfecta.*[31]

Here, the whole emerges as even more important than the *telos* of the individual parts that make it up. At the same time, we must remember that Aquinas states this explicitly only for *natural things*. Given the principle "*ars imitatur naturam*" and seeing that human reason proceeds from simple things to composite things just as from imperfect to perfect things, we can reasonably conclude that the human community is also an end, and that the individual human being is merely a means to achieving that end.

---

30 *In Octo Libros Politicorum Aristotelis Expositio*, n. 4. "Since therefore human reason must make use not only of those things that men seek to make use of, but also the men themselves who are governed according to reason [...] it will arrange a multitude of men into a certain community."

31 *Ibid.*, n. 3. "Nature proceeds from simple things to composite things in such a way that among those things that come about as a result of nature, that which is most composite is also most perfect and constitutes the finality and end of other things, as is plainly seen in any totality with respect to its parts. So also the operative reason of men proceeds from simple things to composite things as from imperfect things to perfect things."

Aquinas, however, though logically sound, never explicitly entertains a conclusion of this type. It will be interesting to see why.

As will become clearer in the course of our study, there is a strong anti-individualistic element that emerges in Aquinas and Aristotle primarily for systematic reasons: In every consideration of nature, the whole is more important than the part, and it is virtually always legitimate to sacrifice the "rights" of one of the parts for the well-being of the whole. In the classical tradition there are instances in which a certain part of the whole is placed in competition with—and even opposition to—the whole. As a paradigmatic example, we might take Socrates's argument in the *Apology* that the wise man has the duty to remain faithful to a truth that is more powerful than him and binds him to a political community.[32] To this same branch will be grafted the fundamental Christian idea that man possesses an immortal soul and therefore bears a resemblance to God, making him a single spiritual substance endowed with greater dignity than the entire human species (if we consider it a natural species). From another point of view there is a strong dose of individualism in Aristotle's thought which, to a certain degree, is due to a polemic directed against abstract generality.[33] Unlike Plato's *Republic*, the Aristotelian *polis* does not allow for the type of unity that would abolish the intermediate communities that make it up. The whole is certainly worth more than the part, but only insofar as it encompasses the rights of the part. Finally, just as art imitates nature but cannot equal it, so the totalities constructed by art are different from those constructed by nature; in some ways the former more closely approximates the perfect totality than the latter. As a totality with a natural basis, but which nevertheless rests upon art for its adequate completion, the ontological status of the city-state is very different from that of the human person; and, as we shall see, it cannot entirely absorb the human person into itself.

32   In the *Crito,* however, Socrates defends the right of the city-state against the arbitrary will of the individual. The subject must obey in all matters except when the salvation of one's soul is at stake; i.e., the highest level of obedience is owed to the truth.

33   This is the reason for the entire anti-Platonic polemic in Aristotle. See *Politics,* 1263b, 30 ff.

How these two elements—the anti-individualistic and the individual-istic—are reconciled and integrated by Aquinas is what we will shall try to ascertain in what follows. To do this, we must first put ourselves in direct contact—almost verbatim—with Aquinas's commentary on Aristotle.

3. The Aristotelian-Thomistic notion of the city-state

At the beginning of his summary of Book I of the *Politics,* Aquinas once more discusses the city-state's nature and addresses the question of how it might be considered a totality.[34] He begins by saying that the city-state must be considered a teleological whole, organized for the purpose of some good. The city-state comes about as the result of man's activity and is thus to be treated philosophically as a human work (i.e., an art). Moreover, every human action aims at some good, be it real or anticipated. The city-state therefore exists for the sake of some good, but it is also good in itself. How will we rank this good among the various goods toward which human action is directed? Naturally, as the highest. The city-state is, in fact, the most important community because it contains within itself every other community. It embraces and safeguards other important human goods. In fact, the city-state "*intendit* [. . .] *bonum commune*," which is a higher and more divine good than the good of the individual.[35] This affirmation will be reinforced by what Aquinas says later in the commentary:

> *Sic igitur patet, quod totum est prius naturaliter quam partes materiae, quamvis partes sint priores ordine generationis. Sed singuli homines comparantur ad totam civitatem, sicut partes hominis ad hominem. Quia sicut manus aut pes non potest esse sine homine, ita nec unus homo est per se sufficiens ad vivendum separatus a civitate.*[36]

---

34 Thomas begins with the *divisio textus* and then proceeds to their *expositio.* That is, he first shows the conceptual articulation of the passage and then gives a paraphrase of it.

35 *In Octo Libros Politicorum Aristotelis Expositio*, n. 11. See also the *Nicomachean Ethics,* 1894a, 18.

36 *Ibid.*, n. 39. "It is therefore evident that the whole has priority over the material

Man is not self-sufficient in such a way that he can live completely apart from the human community. If he tries to live such radical independence, he will turn himself into a brute insofar as he cuts off those interconnections that make him properly human. Or instead, he will end up resembling a god as he tries to find within himself an adequate substitute for those specifically human needs.

How should we understand Aquinas's emphasis on the social nature of human living? And just what are the specific human needs that can be satisfied only within the community we call a city-state? We find an initial hint of Aquinas's response in his criticism of those who equate the city-state with the household by arguing that the only difference between them is quantitative, so that a city-state is nothing other than a large household and a household nothing other than a small city-state. Aquinas, relying on Aristotle, rejects this position since the respective elements that make up the household and city-state are different. The household—that is, the family—together with the associations of kinship and neighborliness related to it, are the constitutive elements that make up the larger reality called the city-state. These smaller communities are its natural elements such that the city-state is not simply a collection of individuals but an ordered whole built from families and intermediate communities. The underlying principle of the organic process that leads to the existence of the city-state is the primordial insufficiency of the single individual, rendering him incapable of living well if he is not in communication with other people. The most basic network of communication between human beings is found in the family unit. At the basis of the family is the unity of a man and a woman. This, therefore, is the first element of the city-state: *"quia oportet nos dividere civitatem usque ad partes minimas, necesse est dicere quod prima combinatio est personarum quae sine invicem esse non possunt, scilicet maris et feminae."*[37]

parts, even though the parts come first from a temporal point of view [...]. Individual men, however, stand in relation to the whole of the city-state just as the parts of man stand in relation to man as a whole. In fact, just as the hand or the foot cannot exist without the man, so no man is capable of living by himself separated from the city-state." The corresponding text in the *Politics* is 1253a, 25–29.

37 *Ibid.*, n. 17. "Since we must divide the city-state into its smallest elements, we must say that the first combination is that of persons who cannot exist reciprocally without one another, which is the combination of a man and a woman."

This first form of communication is not the result of a conscious human decision; reason rather gravitates toward it by recognizing the self-evident order provided by nature. This attraction is rooted in the desire to fill the world with progeny similar to oneself, which is the way of preserving the species and ensuring that the individual can participate in a kind of immortality.

The second natural relationship—which is also a relationship of "communication" and a fundamental component of the city-state—is between master and slave. Aquinas roots this relationship in the necessity of labor: "*Natura enim non solum intendit generationem, sed etiam quod generata salventur.*"[38] .The care necessary to ensure that the product of generation will survive requires human labor, and different people take part in this labor in different ways. The wise man, gifted with foresight and the ability to organize his activities in such a way that they produce what is good and eliminate what is evil, will have a directive role. Someone with physical strength but lacking wisdom will look out for himself and make his own contribution to society through his material and physical powers. The relationship between a man and a woman is different from that between master and slave since reproduction is the aim of the former but labor the latter. Reproduction and labor are qualitatively distinct activities that entail qualitatively distinct human relationships, even if the "barbarians" are incapable of comprehending this. At this point, Aquinas elaborates an interesting explanation about the meaning of the word "barbarian." There is no such digression in the Aristotelian text, but for Aquinas it reinforces the importance of communication as the basis for social order.

A barbarian has a limited capacity for communication. In a more immediate and proximate sense, a barbarian is someone who does not speak our language and, because of this deficiency, is impeded from communicating with us. In an absolute sense, however, a barbarian is someone who, generally speaking, is incapable of speaking because he participates in the universal language of reason only in a limited and imperfect way. The barbarian is thus considered a "foreigner" (relatively speaking) to the human community; he is a "slave" by nature. The signs of barbarism are the inability

---

38   *Ibid.*, n. 19. "Nature in fact wants not only generation, but the survival of the fruits of generation."

to legislate a rational law for oneself, to write, and to exercise more refined communicative skills that give birth to literacy: "*barbaries convenienter hoc signo declaratur, quod homines vel non utuntur legibus vel irrationabilibus utuntur: et similiter quod apud aliquas gentes non sint exercitia literarum.*"[39]

The family, therefore, stands at the intersection of two types of personal communication. The first is directed toward procreation and the second toward work. The community that emerges as a result of these channels of communication is the backdrop for daily human life. The community of the neighborhood, based on material proximity and bonds of kinship, calls for a kind of mutual exchange that is no longer ordinary or restricted to the most basic needs. As a family grows and extends, it gradually submits itself to the wise counsel of its elders. When this is passed on from one generation to the next in a strictly hereditary way, we see the formation of a monarchical/patriarchal rule.

Finally, the city-state is also composed of a certain number of neighborhood communities. These are established to foster human living so that it flourishes as much as possible. It allows for a more perfect division of labor as well as more intricate networks of human communication in such a way that the members of a community not only survive but live well—that is, humanly. If the original motive for the coalescence of neighborhoods into a city-state is to survive, then the very existence of the city-state provides the basis for moving to the next level: living well and living humanly.

> *Est enim de ratione civitatis, quod in ea inveniantur omnia quae sufficiunt ad vitam humanam* [...] *est* [...] *primitus facta gratia vivendi, ut scilicet homines sufficienter invenirent unde vivere possent: sed ex eius esse provenit, quod homines non solum vivant, sed quod bene vivant, inquantum per leges civitatis ordinatur vita hominum ad virtutes.*[40]

---

39 *Ibid.*, n. 23. "The barbarian is sufficiently recognizable from this fact: that men either do not make use of laws or have irrational laws; and equally from the fact that among some people there is no phenomenon of literature."

40 *Ibid.*, n. 31. "It belongs in fact to the concept of the city-state that within it are found all that is necessary for human life [...]. The city-state is in fact established first of all for the art of living—that is so that men can find their

We can therefore say that the city-state is the context in which human beings learn to practice virtue and cultivate their very humanity. The city-state is the only setting in which this can occur in the most compete way. Thus, the city-state is not merely a collection of individuals but a dimension of the human spirit. By his very nature, in fact, man is an *animal civile*.

The proof for this is given by the fact that man uses words—namely, he has the gift of language. Other animals in fact make use of their *vox* for communicating sadness or joy, but man alone possesses *loquutio*:

> *Sed loquutio humana significat quid est utile et quid nocivum. Ex quo sequitur quod significet iustum et iniustum [...] Et ideo loquutio est propria hominibus; quia hoc est proprium eis in comparatione ad alia animalia, quod habeant cognitionem boni et mali, ita et iniusti, et aliorum huiusmodi, quae sermone significari possunt.*[41]

Language is available to man as a means for him to express the truth about good and evil. The phenomenon of the city-state bears witness to the entire network of communicative relations by which man brings about good and evil in his own life in a rational way as he strives to live according to a truth known and made manifest to him through relationships with others. Human beings therefore build the city-state because they are driven by the same natural impulse that motivates them to live according to virtue. In fact, the human being is simultaneously the best and the worst of animals. His intellectual and moral capacities may be directed to justice and goodness but they may also turn toward injustice and evil. In the latter case, human beings are the most powerful and ferocious of beasts. They thus find it necessary to live according to a law that will lead them to the good. This need is in turn fulfilled only by their own efforts. The fact that man is

adequate sustenance; from the city-state's existence, however, derives the fact that men not only live, but live well; insofar as the life of man, from the laws of the city-state, are ordered to the virtues."

41 *Ibid.*, n. 37. "Human language indicates that which is useful and that which is harmful. From this it follows that language also indicates what is just and unjust [...]. Therefore, language is proper to men; in fact, men, unlike other animals, possess knowledge of good and evil, and in this way also of the unjust and of other such things which can be expressed through discourse."

an *animal civile* does not mean that he has always automatically lived in a city-state, nor that he lives in a just and well-ordered city-state. Rather, as human beings we must fully and freely embrace the task of building up the city-state so that it exists in this way. This is a task that can only be performed by human beings.

4. Some critical observations

A comprehensive overview of the Aristotelian/Thomistic text as explained thus far reveals a few initial responses to the problems outlined at the beginning. But several new problems also arise.

The principle of totality has been vigorously affirmed, even if this totality seems, in the modern context, to be oddly opposed to the individual, subjugating him to the whole; at same time, totality is both an effect of—and a condition for—that particular opening of the personality that comes through virtuous living. The city-state is truly a city-state only to the extent that it respects and safeguards the family and the intermediate communities within it and recognizes their respective rights. If it were to impose itself on the family and other intermediate communities as an undifferentiated, all-consuming, and oppressive totality, it would cease to be an authentic city-state.

This is the impetus for Aristotle's polemic against Plato's *Republic*.[42] Aristotle holds that the purpose of the city-state is to make the virtuous life possible. If it wants to retain its proper and specific essence, the city-state can never squelch the search for truth or thwart the citizens' pursuit of a virtuous life. Moreover, it is equally true that human beings cannot live according to virtue if they are isolated from one other. Here we find ourselves, albeit in a slightly different context, in the same paradoxical situation represented by the dialogue between Socrates and the laws in the *Crito*.[43] Socrates does not wish to challenge the laws that have condemned him to death. As a citizen, he is fully aware of his duty towards the city-state,

---

42 This occupies a major section of the *Politics,* bk. 2. Aquinas also makes numerous references to this topic. See *In Octo Libros Politicorum Aristotelis Expositio*, n. 172–255.

43 Plato, *Crito,* n. 50.

because without the city-state he would never have been able to acquire the very moral character that made it possible for him to challenge the city-state. On the other hand, strict fidelity to his moral character (and by means of his character to the city-state itself) prevents Socrates from obeying an unjust law since to do so would destroy not only his moral character but the very *raison d'être* of the city-state.

Insofar as it is a communicative totality, the city-state is based on truth. At the same time, man—as the subject of communication—can just as easily direct himself to falsehood as to truth. The city-state can also introduce a regime of false communication, hence the need to order the city-state according to the rule of reason. Another element that merits particular attention in Aquinas's commentary is labor. It is here that we encounter the problem of slavery, which we will look at more thoroughly later, but we also encounter two other important issues to which we now turn our attention.

First of all, work is strictly tied to the family. In fact, the family is the specific reason for work and the very context in which work is performed. The latter of these notions seems extraordinary to us today. The family is no longer the primary unit in which work is carried out. It has been replaced by the new realities of the factory and the office which, of course, were not included in Aristotle's considerations. From this perspective, the Aristotelian/Thomistic treatment of work initially seems insufficient and perhaps even superficial. It remains to be seen if and how the spatial and chronological transformation of the places and times for "family" and the places and times for "work" will definitively sever the moral connection between the two. Perhaps the Aristotelian/Thomistic position needs to be tweaked rather than completely overturned. Could it be that the problems we associate with work are due to a fundamental lack of understanding of what "work" really means in the wake of its compartmentalization from other human experiences necessarily connected to it and which give it deeper meaning?[44]

Secondly, both Aristotle and Aquinas connect the topic of work to language and communication. They do this in two ways: First, work is not merely the transformation of the external world but a communicative

44   See Józef Tischner, *Etica del lavoro* (Bologna: CSEO, 1982).

relationship with other human persons; secondly, the institution of slavery is based on a deficiency of communicative ability that makes the slave incapable of participating in the city-state's wider working community in a direct and autonomous way. He must therefore be inserted into it and have his behaviors regulated within it by another party.

5. The problem of slavery

Is it theoretically just for one human being to become the slave of another? Insofar as slavery was a well-established social institution enjoying respectability and a high level of social consensus at the time of Aristotle, both he and Aquinas present the problem in unambiguous terms:

> *Alia opinio est, quod habere servum sit praeter naturam, et quod sola lege sit ordinatum quod quidam sunt servi et quidam liberi, et quod nulla differentia sit inter eos secundum naturam. Unde ulterius inducunt quod est iniustum esse aliquos servos. Ex quadam enim violentia provenit quod quidam alios sibi subiecerunt in servos.*[45]

In responding to this question, Aquinas first draws attention to the economical indispensability of slavery. A single man cannot bring his ideas and plans to fruition without the help of other men. Ordering a common life according to reason requires several people to work together to realize a plan conceived by only one:

> *Principales enim artifices, qui architectores dicuntur, non indigerent ministris, neque domini domorum indigerent servis, si unumquodque instrumentum inanimatum posset ad imperium domini, agnoscens*

---

45 *In Octo Libros Politicorum Aristotelis Expositio*, n. 49. "The other opinion holds that to own a slave is contrary to nature, and that only by law is it established that some people are slaves and others are free, and that there is no difference between them from the viewpoint of nature. Furthermore, these same people conclude that it is unjust for there to be slaves. Indeed, the fact that some men have subjugated others to themselves is due to a certain type of violence."

*ipsum, perficere opus suum; puta, quod pectines per se pectinarent, et
plectra per se cytharizarent, sicut dicitur de statua quam fecit
Daedalus, quod per ingenium argenti vivi, movebat seipsam.*[46]

Aristotle is fully aware of the material basis for slavery. It is precisely
for this reason that he calls the slave an instrument, but a particular kind
of instrument. In a certain way, all the hermeneutical problems we discussed
above about how to read the Thomistic texts converge precisely on this
point: How is the specificity of the instrument of slavery to be understood?

Moreover, up until this point we have been concerned with an exposition of Aquinas's thought. Nevertheless, at the same time, we have indirectly
engaged in an exposition of Aristotle's thought *through* Aquinas. In fact,
Aquinas carries out the task of paraphrasing Aristotle so assiduously that
he almost never distances himself or diverges from the Stagirite at all. Yet
when he turns his attention to an analysis of the instrumentality of slavery,
we clearly detect a change in emphasis that shows a significant difference
between his thinking and Aristotle's. If we examine the text attentively and
take stock of its full implications, we find that the difference is not superficial or idiosyncratic but substantial to the extent that two entirely different
philosophical positions are formulated. But we cannot simply say that
Aquinas *countered* Aristotle's thought (it would be very hard to defend such
a position in light of Thomas's constant deference and obsequiousness to
Aristotle as evidenced throughout the commentary), but that he rather takes
a decisive stance in opting for one of two possible interpretations of Aristotle that are in fact incompatible and diametrically opposed to one another.

Aquinas's argument begins with a distinction between *factio* and
actio that can be summarized as a difference between transitive and intransitive acts about which we spoke earlier. *Factio* is a transitive act that
effects real change and actually produces an external object. *Actio,*

46   *Ibid.*, n. 52. "The most important artisans—that is, those whom we call ar-
     chitects—would have no need of workers, and masters of households likewise
     would have no need of servants, if each inanimate instrument were capable
     of recognizing the master's signals and performing the necessary task; as would
     be the case if combs could comb themselves and stringed instruments could
     pluck themselves, as is reported about the statue sculpted by Daedelus—for
     it moved by itself from the effect of the living silver from which it was made."

however, is intransitive and remains internal to the person. Even though the slave performs tasks that lead him to alter some external reality through brute force, and even though this is the basis for the legitimacy of slavery, Aquinas takes the slave's activity as an *actio* and not a *factio*. This derives from the fact that the slave is not located within an inter-communicative context while performing his work. In fact, *"actio et factio differunt specie [...]. Sed vita, idest conversatio domestica, non est factio sed actio: ergo servus est minister et organum eorum quae pertinent ad actionem, non autem eorum quae pertinent ad factionem."*[47]

In short, a slave is not the subject of autonomous *actio*. He is related to his master as sheer property. He is not "the master's slave" in the same way the master is "the slave's master" since the slave belongs to the master completely. It is precisely in this that we see a difference between the slave and those who are poor, those who are free but miserable, and those who are paid for their work. All of latter may be another person's instrument for accomplishing a determined task. They may all be slaves in this sense. But their entire humanity is not exhausted in their servitude. As soon as the working hours are over and they change out of their work clothes, salaried employees lead a perfectly normal, free, domestic life. But slaves do nothing but render service to their masters and are symmetrically related to them only insofar as their service corresponds directly to the master's needs. In other words, the slave belongs to the master *as man*. Aristotle thus concludes his argument with a definition of a slave: The slave is "a possessed thing [...] an active and separated organ."[48]

---

47   *Ibid.*, n. 53. "'To act' and 'to make' are of different species [...]. But life—that is, domestic communication—is not a 'to do'; the slave, therefore, is a servant and instrument of those things that concern acting, not making." The Aristotelian terms corresponding to *factio* and *actio* are *poiēsis* and *praxis* respectively.

48   *Politics,* 1254b, 16–17. "[K]tēma *di organon praktikon kai chōriston.*" This opens up an extremely important philological question. In fact, the text provided by Ross carries the phrase just quoted, *"allou d'estin anthrōpos hos an ktēma ē anthrōpos ōn,"* which is followed, after a comma, by *"ktēma de organon praktikon kai choriston."* Such a reading weakens, and even places into doubt, a significant difference between Aquinas and Aristotle. In any case, it is difficult to understand Ross's option. Many *codices,* in fact, have *anthrōpos ōn,*

At this point Aquinas—who hitherto has not swerved from Aristotle's teaching (indeed, he calls him the "master of those who know")—momentarily interrupts his strict paraphrase of Aristotle and states a conclusion well worth citing in its entirety:

> *Unde potest talis definitio servi concludi: servus est organum animatum activum separatum alterius homo existens. In qua quidem definitione, organum ponitur tamquam genus, et adduntur quinque differentiae. Per hoc enim quod dicitur animatum, distinguitur ab instrumentis inanimatis: per hoc autem quod dicitur activum distinguitur a ministro artificis, qui est organum animatum factivum: per hoc autem quod dicitur alterius existens, distinguitur a libero, qui quandoque ministrat in domo, non sicut res possessa, sed sponte vel mercede conductus. Per hoc autem quod dicitur separatum, distinguitur a parte quae est alterius non separata; sicut manus. Per hoc quod dicitur homo existens, distinguitur a brutis animalibus, quae sunt res possessae separatae.*[49]

rather than *doulos ōn*. For example, Berolinensis 397, Ambrosanius 126, Parisinus Coislinianus 161, Parisinus 2026, etc. Codex Γ, on the other hand, reconstructed from William of Moerbeke's version, also has *ē doulos ē*. In any case, even if we accept the reading established by Ross, there is no doubt that the emphasis on the slave's humanity is still well preserved in Aquinas's text but is not in Aristotle's, as is confirmed by a further comparison with Aquinas's other works. We must not forget, however, that the decisive text to comprehend Aquinas's attitude as commentator would be William of Moerbeke's translation—that is, Codex Γ.

49   *In Octo Libros Politicorum Aristotelis Expositio*, n. 55. "We can therefore deduce the following definition of a slave: The slave is an active animated organ separated from another, existing as man. In this definition, organ is taken as the genus, to which five differences are added. The designation 'animated' distinguishes it from inanimate instruments; by 'active,' the slave is distinguished from an artesian, who is a 'fictive' (i.e., *faciens*) animated organ; insofar as it is said that the slave 'exists as the property of another,' he is distinguished from the free person who sometimes serves within a household not as a possessed thing, but rather out of his own willingness or for monetary gain. Insofar as the slave is said to be 'separated,' he is distinguished from the non-separated part of another person, such as a hand. Insofar as he is said to 'exist as man,' the slave is distinguished from brute animals, which are also separate possessed things."

Of these five specific differences, Aristotle lists only two. He says the slave is an "active separated organ." The difference between Aristotle and Aquinas can be explained by the fact that Aquinas adds specific differences that Aristotle mentioned previously but did not give a definitive conclusion. He distinguishes the organs of animated things from inanimate things[50] and then says the slave is *alterius existens*.[51]

It is important to note that the specification *homo existens* is not to be found in Aristotle's text.[52] But Aquinas does not hesitate to go beyond a strict exposition and rearrange the material. Indeed, he goes further. Contrary to his normal practice of rigorously adhering to the role of commentator, he adds something unmistakably his own, something above and beyond the original text. Perhaps Aristotle would have had no objections to Aquinas's addition, but his original interest was undoubtedly the acquisition of a slave as a possessed thing. This seems repugnant to Aquinas's moral sensibilities, who, without contradicting Aristotle, decides to make a significant modification—namely, to consider the slave as a man. We shall see how this integration reveals an important difference between Aristotle and Aquinas on the problem of slavery. At this point, however, I will make just a few preliminary observations.

In the first place, I wish to draw attention to the fact that it would be a serious mistake to read this text exclusively from our modern, libertarian point of view. This would undervalue or overlook the realism of Aristotle's position. Ancient society needed slaves in order to survive. In order for some people to devote undivided attention to art and culture and others to governing the city-state and to creating the necessary conditions for continued progress, it was absolutely necessary that some people provide for the material needs of civic life by using their bodily strength. This may strike us as repulsive today, but it was nonetheless a strict material necessity. As we shall see, by the time the Church articulated the doctrine that each human being is essentially free, it was not able to change the state of affairs

---

50 *Politics*, 1253b, 32. "[O] doulos ktēma ti emphuchon."
51 *Politics* 1254a, 12–13. "[H]o de doulos ou monon desmotou doulos estin, alla kai olōs ekeinou."
52 Or at the very least—if we accept Ross' reading—we would not find it with the same intensity and import as we do in Aquinas's paraphrase.

by waving a magic wand. We could even say that the task of transforming the material conditions of life to make it possible for each human being to develop his or her capacity to become entirely free will endure to the end of time. There are types of labor that impede the full development of man's authentic human sensibilities and the intellectual and rational faculties necessary for his freedom, but these types of labor are nonetheless indispensable for social stability. As cynical as Aristotle's solution to the problem may seem, we cannot close our eyes to the problem. In more recent times Nietzsche severely stigmatized Christian morality and upright moral living, claiming we could do away with the problem altogether.[53]

In our own time, the automation of technical and industrial means of production partly alleviates the problem. Automation makes it possible for combs to comb and stringed instruments to play without players, but it also gives rise to other problems. As we shall see, in order to be free it is not enough to be free from servile work; it is also necessary that we know how to master ourselves.[54]

Insofar as Aristotle limits his discussion to showing that slavery is necessary for economic order, he argues that slavery is useful but not necessarily just. Slavery would be natural and just only if it turns out that the master's need of "animated instruments" for carrying out his domestic duties can effectively be satisfied only through the use of humans who, in carrying out this function, simultaneously fulfill their own interior needs and attain their spiritual destiny.

Above all, to be subject to servile conditions, a person must be completely incapable of governing himself: "*ille est naturaliter servus, qui habet aptitudinem naturalem ut sit alterius, inquantum scilicet non potest regi*

---

53   Nietzsche does not believe the problem can be solved. Thus he opts to return to a "master morality" in order to avoid the decline and fall of civilization. The position is perfectly consistent with his denial of the person's transcendence through work—a transcendence that Aquinas affirms—and, on the other hand, his lack of faith in a utopian future in which a perfect social organization would obviate the need for servile work. See *The Gay Science*, a. 329.

54   Consequently, the man incapable of mastering himself will remain a slave by nature even in a situation where there is no economic necessity for the existence of slavery.

propria ratione, per quam homo est dominus sui."[55] Be that as it may, a slave's lack of reason never reduces him to the level of brute animals. He too participates in rationality, not insofar as he himself possesses rational knowledge, but insofar he is able to participate in rational knowledge by being led by another *(edoctus ab alio)*. A slave's reason is therefore passive, capable only of receiving that which the free man—i.e. the man of wisdom—teaches him.

Can we not also say that there are human beings who enjoy a similar limited participation in the life of reason? From a purely empirical viewpoint, it is not difficult to see that this is indeed the case. Throughout their lives, many people move and act not according to reason but only through the impulse of immediate stimuli arising from sensuality and emotions. It would not be out of line to say that it might be better for such people to be directed and ordered by others rather than to leave them to their own inconstancy. Indeed, before being slaves to others, they are slaves to themselves. Aquinas makes this kind of claim when he says that there is a similarity between what happens among human beings and what happens among animals.

.Under the care of human masters, domestic animals are better off than wild animals left to their own devices. In a similar way, it is better for a barbarian to be a slave than to be a free man.[56] From this point of view, slavery is the result of man's incapacity to exercise dominion over himself, i.e., to become master of himself.

If up until now Aristotle's exposition has been fairly persuasive, it also opens up several difficulties. One of these is admitted by Aristotle himself. According to his line of reasoning it is just for the wise man to give commands to the barbarian. However, as is readily evident in the empirical world, it does not always happen that those who are naturally slaves obey those who are naturally free. It is quite often the contrary: Those who are by nature free can be reduced to slavery by those who do not have knowledge

---

55 *In Octo Libros Politicorum Aristotelis Expositio*, n 68. "The one who has a natural attitude of belonging to another is also a slave by nature, insofar as he cannot master himself by his own reason: the usual means by which man masters himself."

56 *Ibid.*, n. 65. See *Politics*, 1254b, 10–15.

of the truth but who nonetheless make ready use of forceful means. Up to this point, Aristotle's demonstration presumes a kind of identification between wisdom and the virtues of warfare, similar to the situation Plato sets up in the *Republic*. If, on the other hand, this strict connection between virtue and force is not permitted, Aristotle's reasoning retains some theoretical rigor but loses much of its practical relevance from the point of view of the legitimization of a universally acceptable social hierarchy. It would be a good thing if the wise were able to master the barbarians, and it would be good for the barbarians to be mastered by the wise,[57] though this does not always happen, and indeed often the opposite is the case.

In order to refute the objection, Aristotle introduces a new justification for the practice of slavery that he articulates in two parts. In the first place, he notes that the custom of having the conquered become the slaves of the conquerors is useful for both the conquerors and the conquered. For in this way the conquerors increase their property, enhance their leisure, and save the lives of the conquered who, if they had not become slaves, would have been exterminated. Secondly, since it is not possible to determine by human law who the wise are—that is, who has the right to govern—it is necessary to refer to some standard of superiority. The superiority of force and victory in battle serve as the criterion for distinguishing freeman from slaves, even though those designated as slaves and those designated free according to the law will not always accord with those who are naturally slaves and those who are naturally free.

In any case, if slavery is unjust in the case of the single individual, it remains nonetheless valid as a social institution. There are, in fact, arts and

57   In any case, we might ask ourselves: In what sense would it be "a good" for the barbarians? Aristotle, in fact, distinguishes between political domination and a despotic domination. In political domination, governance is directed toward the common good of both the governor and the governed. In despotic domination (which is directed toward slaves), governance aims exclusively at the good of the governor. The good of the slave is included in the intention of the governor only to the extent that the slave is a necessary instrument for the master's good, or as a secondary effect of actions performed for his good. Are we thus allowed to presuppose that, in this way, the slave will reach his properly human end? Or does this not imply that the slave's end must be at a lower level than that of free man, at least if we say that the free man's highest end is knowledge of the truth and living according to it?

trades that in a certain sense debilitate physical stamina and exhaust one's spirit. But it is still necessary that some perform these tasks just as it is right that others—using whatever means available—be free of this kind of work and especially from waging war.

A consideration of these passages brings to mind an incisive commentary by Hegel on freedom in the Hellenistic world.[58] The Greeks knew that some individuals were able to live freely: Through the exercise of civic virtue and a love for wisdom, they extract themselves from the universal law of necessity and raise themselves up to the level of authentic freedom. However, the idea that all men are born free by nature is foreign to the classical mind. And yet if human beings are free by coming into contact with the truth, how can we say that the illiterate, the uneducated, and those innocently inhibited by life's circumstances are able to live an authentically human life?[59]

Here, of course, the Aristotelian position clashes with the Christian conviction of the universal call to salvation. From this perspective access to the divine (i.e., that which is preeminently intelligible and desirable in itself) is granted to every human being. According to the Christian teaching on grace it is no longer possible to hold the view that the wise can elevate themselves through their own initiative, strength, and unaided natural faculties. That would contradict the unique character of grace given to them so that they might know God. Moreover, we may not entertain the possibility that someone might be excluded from the gift of grace because of an inferior or defective participation in the human community. The most original form of communication—that which decisively accords with the dignity of the human subject—is communication with God, and the initiative for this communication comes from above. When we consider the infinite distance God has overcome to draw close to man, the social distances separating different categories of men are "spiritually" annihilated.

58   *Encyclopedia of the Philosophical Sciences,* par. 483.
59   Here the temptation is to think that for the illiterate, participation in liberty is limited to participation in the city-state or in the history as governed by the wise man. In this case, the soul of the illiterate person participates in a type of collective immortality for the species but not in an individual immortality; that is, he is not responsible as an individual in the face of truth.

6. Thomas Aquinas's position on slavery

We are now in a better position to understand the significance of Aquinas's insistence that slaves are human beings. Slaves cannot be completely absorbed into the domestic community since they too have the constitutive power to transcend every human community due to their subjective finality as persons. In other words, their finality as persons is nobler than the particular human community in which they live. This conclusion is reinforced by the remaining texts in which Aquinas highlights the problem of slavery.

For our purposes, *Summa Theologiae* II-II, q. 122, a. 4 is particularly relevant. Here, Aquinas asks whether the prohibition of servile work on feast days (particularly the Sabbath) as contained in the Decalogue is a ceremonial or moral precept, and whether it is a positive divine right or natural right. Here is his response:

> [P]raeceptum de sanctificatione sabbati, litteraliter intellectum, est partim morale, partim caeremoniale. Morale quidem, quantum ad hoc quod homo deputet aliquod tempus vitae suae ad vacandum divinis. Inest enim homini naturalis inclinatio ad hoc quod cuilibet rei necessariae deputetur aliquod tempus, sicut corporali refectioni, somno et aliis huiusmodi. Unde etiam spirituali refectioni, qua mens hominis in Deo reficitur, secundum dictamen rationis naturalis aliquod tempus deputat homo. Et sic habere aliquod tempus deputatum ad vacandum divinis, cadit sub praecepto morali.[60]

In this case, being occupied with divine things is clearly a natural inclination and a duty that flows not from divine positive law but from a

---

60 Thomas Aquinas, *Summa theologiae*, II-II, q. 122, a. 4. "[T]he precept to keep the Sabbath holy, understood literally, is partly moral and partly ceremonial. It is moral insofar as it prescribes that each man dedicates a certain time of his life to occupying himself with divine things. In fact, present in every man is the natural inclination to designate a set time for each necessary thing, such as, for example, recreation for the body, sleep, and other things of this type. In the same way, man dedicates a certain amount of time also to spiritual recreation, in which the human mind focuses on God, according to the indication given by natural reason. For this reason, having a certain amount of time designated for divine things falls within the moral precept."

natural right and according to the natural moral law. If every man is *capax Dei*—at least in the sense of being able to accept divine Revelation and of being directed to it through one's capacity to grasp the preambles of faith intellectually—then it is necessary that this universal human property be reflected in the material organization of life. Consequently, we can no longer say that the slave belongs to his master in his entire being. Belonging to God, as something more foundational than belonging to any earthly master, establishes a certain "unavailability" of the slave's personhood even with respect to the master. On the other hand, seeing as he is capable of the highest act of human reason—that is, of being in a relationship with God—it would be difficult to view the slave as incapable of mastering himself according to his own reason in an absolute sense.

Such an incapacity, which Aquinas does not intend to deny completely, will be understood in the particular sense as the incapacity to govern oneself in the material affairs of everyday life. Aquinas thus restricts the inequality of servant and master, an inequality that Aristotle never completely rejected nor placed into serious doubt. In a certain sense, the "slave" and the "wise man" are internally present within each and every individual human being. This is precisely why Aquinas's next claim appears quite reasonable: "*est autem homo alterius servus non secundum mentem sed secundum corpus.*" This is the extreme opposite of Aristotle's position that the servant belongs to the master in an asymmetrical relationship—not only as regards his function as slave but also in his entire self.[61] If we accept Aquinas's position, then there is no longer a qualitative, radical difference between a slave and a free person who serves for monetary gain or some other purpose.

A necessary consequence of this development in Aquinas's thinking will be that the slave, insofar as he is a man, will enjoy a set of rights that belong to him by his very nature, regardless of his social status. For example, Aquinas derives from this the slave's right to contract marriage or to exercise similar natural rights. He writes in the *Summa Theologiae*:

> Et ideo in his quae pertinent ad interiorem motum voluntatis, homo
> non tenetur homini obedire, sed solum Deo. Tenetur autem homo

---

61   See the *Politics*, 1254a, 12–13, and Thomas Aquinas, *In Octo Libros Politico-rum Aristotelis Expositio*, n. 54.

*homini obedire in his quae exterius per corpus sunt agenda. In quibus
tamen etiam, secundum ea quae ad naturam corporis pertinent, homo
homini obedire non tenetur, sed solum Deo, quia omnes homines
natura sunt pares, puta in his quae pertinent ad corporis
sustentationem et prolis generationem.* [62]

The retrieval of man's moral liberty—of his interior dimension—is
hardly without relevance in the sphere of external action. The connection
between body and soul is essential insofar as the soul can only be respected
if its higher dignity is somehow reflected in the external autonomy granted
the person. How this might be defined, and what its minimal limit might
be, are questions that Aquinas does not elaborate. Nevertheless, it is reasonable to think that these questions were percolating under the surface
and would be developed more fully when social circumstances had sufficiently changed. In any case, the fundamental principle formulated by
Aquinas remains the same: "*omnes homines natura sunt pares.*"[63]

So what will this new notion of slavery look like within Aquinas's revised conceptual framework?

In short, slavery will be viewed as a punishment for sin.[64] Man is free
by nature, but he can renounce his freedom by committing sin. Sin is thus
primarily considered as the effect and cause of one's incapacity for self-pos-
session and self-mastery. Because of sin, man can no longer contain his im-
pulses or order himself according to reason. He has become the slave of his
own passions. In such a state slavery can be an effective medicinal punishment for him: punishment insofar as it cuts him off from a fundamental
human good, but medicinal insofar as his master's discipline compensates
for his lack of self control and thus helps him to regain mastery over the irrational part of his soul. We may further conclude that the master may not
give commands to his slave merely in view of his own good as if the slave

---

62 *Summa theologiae*, II-II, q. 104, a. 5. "[I]n that which regards the interior mo-
tives of the will, man is not held to obey man but only God; in fact, all men
are equal by nature; for example, in the things that regard the sustenance of
the body and the generation of offspring."
63 *Summa theologiae*, supplementum, q. 52.
64 See *Summa theologiae*, I-II, q. 94, a. 5, ad 3; 2–2, q. 183, a. 4c; 3, q. 46, a. 3,
ad 3; 3, q. 48, a. 4 ad 2; 3, q. 48, a. 4, ad 2; 3, q. 49, a. 2c.

were merely an instrument. While actualizing his own good thanks to the services provided by the slave, the master must see to it that the slave simultaneously actualizes his own good—not only *qua* slave, but as a human person.[65] All the more so should the master avoid placing obstacles that would prevent the slave from actualizing his own good. To the extent that he does set up obstacles, he violates the slave's fundamental rights.

Aquinas seems to temper the rigor of Aristotle's theory of slavery by means of, on the one hand, considerations taken from Stoic moral philosophy and, on the other hand, considerations distinctive to the Old Testament.[66] Slavery is found in the latter, but it is predominantly a juridical institution regulated by law to prevent harm to the fundamental freedom that belongs to the children of Israel by the will of God.[67] Above all, as noted previously, there is also a Christian anthropology that considers men and woman as essentially free beings and consequently persons both *sui iuris* and *alteri incommunicabilis.* In any case, just as slavery is always relative to sin insofar as it injures human nature without eliminating it, so slavery as a social institution always remains relative in that it must respect the inner sanctuary of the person.

7. Some conclusions

Let us turn to reconsider the questions that sparked our investigation. We were interested in delineating the exact meaning of *ars* and the relationship between the *totum* and the individual subject.

With regard to the latter problem, we can say that the individual subject can never be absorbed completely into the political community. Given that the slave cannot be a mere "*pars civitatis*"—since, as *homo existens,* he has the ability to transcend the community in which he lives—then even more so can he never be absorbed into the city-state. A person cannot belong to the city-state "*secundum se totum.*" The most radical type of belonging that gives rise to man's moral life is his belonging to God. His

---

65   See *Summa theologiae* II-II, q. 57, a. 3, ad 3 and a. 4, ad 2.
66   See Seneca, *De beneficiis,* bk. 3, chap. 20, cited in *Summa theologiae,* II-II, q. 104, a. 5c.
67   See Deut. 15:12.

membership in the city-state is derivative and secondary. Moreover, the reason Aquinas gives for the existence of slavery is the same reason he gives for the existence of the city-state. Man needs a rule to guide his relationship to other men since, on the one hand, he must communicate with them to attain his unique end as a human being, and, on the other, he is tempted to construct these communicative relationships in a way that ignores truth.

Thomistic political philosophy therefore attempts to integrate man into the city-state without having him be completely absorbed by it.

Can we say that there is a clash between Thomistic philosophy and Aristotelian philosophy? This is a complex and daunting question that will allow for no easy answer. In Aristotle we have a kind of oscillation in regard to man's ultimate end. From one point of view, it seems man's ultimate end consists in the contemplation of truth; from another it seems to consist in the exercise of civic virtue. If his ultimate end consists in the practice of civic virtue then his entire destiny is wrapped up in his participation in the life of the city-state. Conversely, if he attains his end primarily in contemplation then the wise man capable of contemplation has an end that transcends the city-state; in a certain sense, the ultimate purpose of the city-state is to give the wise man room for contemplation.

Depending on how one chooses between these "two poles"—both of which are possible interpretations of Aristotle—we will have either to accept or to reject the idea that the human subject has an end above and beyond the city-state.[68] Hence it would not be off the mark to say that Aquinas's solution resolves a problem Aristotle left unresolved. In any case, it is necessary to point out that for Aristotle, as already noted, it is at most only the wise man who, striving to attain his contemplative end, transcends the practical end of the city-state. Aquinas understands contemplation in a more existential sense so that it becomes the proper end of everyone. In this sense there is a difference between Aristotle and Aquinas. But it would be wrong to think that Aquinas's modification of Aristotle is due only to divine revelation with no philosophical basis. As we have seen, the obligation to turn

---

68   See the conclusion of Book 10 of the *Nicomachean Ethics,* where we find what is perhaps the most mature formulation of the Stagirite's thought on this topic. On the one hand, contemplation is the highest end; on the other, it cannot be had outside of a well-ordered city-state.

one's soul to God is a natural—not a revealed—moral obligation, such that the potential to do so is a natural potential. Indeed, this is confirmed by the Thomistic idea of a *desiderium naturale videndi Deum*.[69]

We must determine more precisely the meaning of *ars* as Aquinas uses it in the Prologue. It should now be fairly clear that if we understand *ars* as work, we accept a position that goes beyond the Aristotelian conception of art and work since such a conception implies an absolute separation between manual and intellectual labor, as Aristotle himself held and emphasized numerous times in the *Politics*. In any case, while we cannot go so far as to say that Aquinas completes the process of unifying art and work, there is little doubt that art and work are more closely interrelated for him than for Aristotle. This unification necessarily follows upon the clear recognition of a slave's humanity and his capacity for transcendence. For as much as Aquinas views manual work as a punishment for sin, he also acknowledges its medicinal character to ward off sin and to keep bodily passions at bay, and therefore its capacity to build up one's personal interiority and morality.

Aquinas in fact is driven in this direction by his unique religious vocation. All mendicant orders, including Aquinas's Dominicans, bore the brunt of accusations in Paris during his lifetime with regard to the alleged incompatibility of a contemplative vocation (i.e., the wise man's vocation to transcend whatever circumstances in which he happens to find himself) and manual work. Manual work, which the mendicant orders were required to perform in certain circumstances, was considered unworthy of the cleric and incompatible with his vocation.

On the other hand, among the mendicant orders there was a tendency to consider manual work as absolutely obligatory, culminating in an interdict against non-manual work and any attempt to broaden one's culture. In his struggle to refute both claims, Aquinas affirms, on the one hand, manual work's compatibility with contemplation, and, on the other hand, the unified nature of human work, such that the obligation to "work" may be fulfilled both by performing intellectual work and by performing manual work.[70]

---

69   Cf. *Summa theologiae*, I-II, qq. 1–5.

70   *Summa theologiae*, II-II, q. 187, a. 3; *Quodlibetales*, 7, q. 7; *Contra retrahentes*, c. 16; *Contra impugnantes*, cc. 5–6; *Summa contra gentiles*, 3, c. 135; *In Iohannem*, c. 6, 1.3.

Finally, our investigation leads us to highlight the enormous contemporary relevance of the Aristotelian/Thomistic formulation. Aquinas gives consideration to—and ultimately accepts—the concept of totality as a useful methodological tool for understanding human reality. This allows us to make use of several elements of Hegel's philosophy of history in which the concept of totality is absolutely central. Aquinas, however, does not move from a methodological conception to a metaphysical/immanentist conception of totality. If understanding the structure and implications of a given historical phenomenon is facilitated by the category of totality, then the human subject transcends every totality and inevitably faces an unavoidable ethical responsibility.

An analogous situation holds for the concepts of art and work. As the subject of art, "man" is able to create himself, the city-state, and the sphere of human values. Nevertheless, human creative activity is always secondary insofar as it is carried out against the backdrop of divine creation and constantly connected with the task of "reproducing" within world history the collection of objective values imbedded in the world of nature, and especially in the physical-spiritual nature of the human being.

Finally, our study leads to the hypothesis that there is a line of philosophical reflection culminating in Hegel and Marx that rightfully may be conceived as a developing interpretation of Aristotle, which—with respect to the two decisive questions we have dealt with here—follows a line of choices directly opposed to those made by Aquinas. If this is the case, then we might very well consider Aquinas's reading of Aristotle an *ante-litteram* critique of those later philosophical developments.

Part II
Metaphysics of Knowledge and Politics
in St. Thomas Aquinas

Introduction

In general, a study of Aquinas's political philosophy should begin with the writings that are explicitly political in scope, although we must not forget to frame them within the larger context of his overall system.

The essential reference points for such a study are Aquinas's *De regimine principum,* Questions 90–96 of Parts I and II of the *Summa Theologiae*—together with corresponding passages from the *Summa Contra Gentiles* and the *Commentary on the Sentences of Peter Lombard*—as well as the *Commentary on Aristotle's Politics,* although the latter text is used less frequently due to particular difficulties in its interpretation. From these texts, we can draw a more or less articulated, global vision of Aquinas's political thought. The reasons for proceeding in this way are plain enough. These passages effectively constitute the collection of Aquinas's political texts, and it seems only natural to turn to them if we want to reconstruct his political thought. It is somewhat unfortunate that politics constitutes only a small portion of his enormous output, although the historical and systematic reasons for this are apparent enough. In any case, we have no way of getting around this limitation.

The method I will use is based on a different presupposition. In the first place, I will try to make use of and thoroughly investigate the systematic connections between Aquinas's political thought and other philosophical areas which he reflected on at greater length. In this way I will delineate the fundamental categories and concepts most relevant to the present study or at least those that emerge as most significant from Aquinas's political texts. We know that Aquinas, following Aristotle, considered politics the apex of practical philosophy. So it is no surprise to discover that many of the ethical concepts he developed have their roots in his political philosophy. We must therefore keep his ethics constantly in view, especially his "general" ethics. Moreover, the notions of politics and political philosophy as developed in the modern era are quite different from those of the thirteenth century. Ever since Hegel, modern thought has established a strict connection between the theory of knowledge and political theory. This connection is reflected in more recent Thomistic philosophy which must address questions that were unforeseeable at the time Aquinas was writing. Here we will offer a critical account of Aquinas's systematic framework and ascertain whether its creative development in the face of modern thought might allow us to bring together, in a surprisingly fruitful way, philosophical disciplines that were clearly distinct in their original systematic framework and therefore never considered contiguous.

To take but one example, in one way or another all of Aquinas's political philosophy is founded on his anthropology. A painstakingly accurate reconstruction of his anthropology is therefore indispensable for a correct understanding of his political philosophy. On the surface, it would seem that an adequate reconstruction of this anthropology presents no particular difficulties. We would simply have to read the *De homine* section of the *Summa Theologiae*. However, one searches in vain for a full development of the fundamental concept of *persona* in this tract. And if we misunderstand this concept, not only will we have an entirely inaccurate anthropology but an inaccurate political philosophy as well. If we want to find the preliminary groundwork for Aquinas's essential anthropology, we must turn to his tract on the Trinity, and only in light of that will we arrive at a more complete understanding of the way he develops his anthropology in the *De homine* of the *Summa Theologiae*. We should also note that Aquinas's angelology has played an extremely important role in the development of anthropology and the philosophy of history through the centuries.

Could we say that Aquinas was confused about—or lacked respect for—the rule of scientific explanation? Such a charge would be both presumptuous and foolish. Anyone with the patience to delve deeply into Aquinas's system will discover an unparalleled coherence and structure. It is also true that such a high level of systematic rigor is uncommon today, meaning that every discipline tends to present itself as an independent, self-

sufficient whole. Hence political philosophy cannot presume its presuppositions are universally known or accepted. The very cultural pluralism that
typifies our present condition would not allow for it. Thus political philosophy is forced to appropriate presuppositions taken from other philosophical disciplines and to justify, mobilize, and defend them as its own.
Conversely, the very same necessity is imposed upon political philosophy
based on the concerns of modern thought—which, as indicated earlier, follows quite a different systematic ordering.

Naturally, I shall not attempt to develop Aquinas's entire political philosophy based on the method described above. Rather, I will limit myself
to a series of observations about his metaphysics of knowledge and its importance for political philosophy. The *leitmotiv* of this study will be a sort
of implicit comparison between Aquinas and Hegel—or better yet, a comparison of Aquinas's philosophy with the modern way of thinking that culminates in Hegel. The idea of a parallelism, together with the idea of a
substantial difference and opposition between Hegel and Aquinas, has already been advanced by Ernst Bloch in a short tract entitled *Avicenne und
die Aristotelische Linke.*[71] According to Bloch there is a palpable continuity
between the naturalistic Aristotelianism of the Middle Ages and the distinctive monism of modern philosophy. The same fundamental theses, by
means of a progressive development and an ever greater awareness of their
revolutionary significance and the ways in which they subvert the existing
order, would eventually pass from Avicenna to Averroës to Siger of Brabant;
from these, through the Aristotelian school of Padua; then to the philosophers of naturalism in Renaissance Italy and Giordano Bruno; and finally
to Hegel and Marx.[72] In his books on German mysticism in the Middle
Ages and the formation of Hegel's thought, another scholar, Galvano della
Volpe—who eventually converted to Marxism—traced a different but analogous journey that runs from Averroës (Aquinas's great adversary in the
thirteenth century) to Hegel, this time passing through Meister Eckhart

71 Ernst Bloch, *Avicenna und die aristotelishe Linke* (Berlin: Suhrkamp Verlag,
    1963).
72 See Bruno Nardi, *Sigieri di Brabante nel pensiero del Rinascimento italiano*
    (Roma: Edizioni Italiane, 1945) and *Saggi sull'aristotelismo padovano dal secolo
    XIV al secolo XVI* (Firenze: Sansoni, 1958).

and his followers rather than through the school of Padova and Italian naturalistic philosophy.[73]

A general survey of this interpretative hypothesis concerning modern thought would seem to legitimize the view that the evolution of modern philosophy amounted to a great debate over how to interpret Aristotle correctly. This debate put naturalistic/gnostic and Thomistic/Christian interpretations face-to-face. I use the designation "Thomistic/Christian" with some hesitation since I am aware of the heated discussion over cultural pluralism and the irreducibility of faith to a single culture or, worse still, a single philosophy. In this case, however, it seems to me that when dealing with Aquinas's philosophy, something even more important than philosophy is at stake. The controversy, as I have tried to describe it, latently implies a millenarian conflict between Gnosticism and Christianity. It seems to me that the fundamental theses of Gnosticism can be reduced to two basic ideas: immanent or pantheistic monism and metaphysical dualism.[74] These are clearly recognizable in the line of thought running from Averroës to Avicenna to Hegel to Marx.[75] Opposed to these are two Christian theses regarding the transcendence of God who became man in Jesus Christ (the theology of the Incarnation and the Trinity), and the original goodness of all things created by God and redeemed by Christ (the philosophy of goodness and being).

The loss of a meaningful distinction between God and man derives from pantheistic Gnostic monism. Man does not become a free and intelligent person through gnosis. He is rather a tiny spark destined to be absorbed into an infinite and impersonal divine light. At the same time, Hegel will assert that man is only one of the infinite facets emanating from the prism of history through which Reason is manifested in the world.

Moreover, metaphysical dualism gives birth to the notion of man's irresponsibility for the good and evil he performs in this life. If in fact

73 See Galvano Della Volpe, *Hegel romantico e mistico* (Firenze: Le monnier, 1929) and *Il misticismo speculativo di Maestro Eckhart nei suoi rapporti storici* (Bologna: Cappelli, 1930).

74 See Emanuele Samek Ludovici, *Metamorfosi della gnosi* (Milano: Ares, 1991).

75 For a reading of modern philosophy in a Gnostic sense, see Augusto Del Noce, *Caratteri Generali del Pensiero Politico Contemporaneo* (Milano: Giuffrè, 1972), pp. 4–100.

personhood is only an illusion, how can the individual be anything more than an epiphenomenon of greater and more objective natural forces that influence his actions, somewhat akin to a puppeteer jostling the strings of his marionettes? Once again, we must note that Christian thought includes two fundamental theses standing at opposite ends of a spectrum: (i) Man is finite and really standing in the presence of an infinite God, and (ii) man is an intelligent and free being, responsible for his own actions, whose destiny God has deigned to place in his own hands.

The comparison between Thomism, on the one hand, and Avicennism and Averroism, on the other (albeit with slightly different shadings in regard to each of their respective philosophical systems), can be carried out at several levels. There is the general doctrine of being, the ability to think about God and spiritual substances, the relationship between the composition of matter/form and substance/being, the distinction between being and essence, and so on. We will at least touch on each of these in what follows. However, the fundamental question that remains at the center of our reflection concerns the unity—or lack thereof—of the human intellect and our way of conceiving it. Even if this question depends heavily on a host of other interconnected questions, it is the hinge upon which the entire debate between Thomism and Averroism has turned throughout history, both in its initial stages at the University of Paris in 1270 and in its subsequent developments down to our own day.

Furthermore, our analysis will not be without a solid theoretical justification. It is on the level of the metaphysics of knowledge that the Gnostic project reaches its completion in the unification-in-distinction between man and God and the negation of personality through the knowing act. Once we give into this, the themes of responsibility and the personal nature of the human act will inevitably collapse. The religious idea of man as finite in himself but nonetheless in need of the infinite, as someone for whom an attitude of dependence and prayer is both natural and primordial, will also crumble.

At this point, it is necessary to say a few words about the controversy of the relationship between Thomism and the philosophy of Pascal. For a long time the dominant trend was to set these two against each other: Aquinas was considered the standard bearer of Christian rationalism built on the foundation of Aristotle, and Pascal was the philosopher of the human heart who rejected the idea that human experience could be circumscribed within an abstract intellectual system.

We must thoroughly revisit and realign the perspective from which we view this opposition. Aquinas was not in fact only an Aristotelian philosopher—he was an original thinker who coherently developed and extended Aristotle's thought in one of several interpretive directions. In this regard he is someone who acknowledges the scientific and philosophical contributions of Aristotle within the fundamental Christian worldview of God's relationship to man. This relationship had already been formulated and developed in an engaging way by Augustine, and would be rediscovered and reformulated by Pascal. The radical problem is the same: How can we defend the fundamental thesis that man has a singular, unique place within the cosmos as he stands at the threshold between the finite and the infinite? How can we articulate his awareness of this finiteness? How can human beings exercise their capacity, precisely on account of that awareness, to place their finiteness into question as they reach toward the infinity of God? In the end, the human aspiration for the infinite and the divine is rooted in the fact that man remains a person, despite every tendency to reduce him to a natural *ens* or to absorb him into the infinite substance of an impersonal, divine mind. From this fundamental perspective emerges the possibility of affirming a certain unity and continuity within Christian philosophy, while at the same time acknowledging its dependence on a legitimate pluralism of emphasis and possible directions for further development beyond its natural dependence on the undeniable originality of its greatest thinkers. It is a continuity that links Augustine to Aquinas, after whom come Pascal and Malebranche in the modern era, followed by Vico and finally Rosmini. In a certain sense, we could say that the entire range of solutions and reflections offered by Aquinas can be gleaned only if retrace the philosophical tradition that stretches back to him and attempts a rigorous but sympathetic comparison of his thought with the thought of modernity.

In a work entitled *La riscoperta del tomismo in Etienne Gilson ed il suo significato presente,* Augusto Del Noce carried out this kind of analysis, focusing on the substantial continuity and harmony between the Thomistic approach and Pascal which he traces by closely examining the *iter* of the latter's thought.[76] Gilson first attempted to isolate a pure Thomistic philosophy on a rational basis, distinct from Aquinas's theology. But after long and arduous study, he ended up denying the possibility of such a "separated" philosophy. His original hypothesis was that Aquinas's philosophical ideas were scattered throughout his writings and could be reassembled independently of theology and faith. A reconstruction of this philosophy seemed crucial for defending Christian philosophy against the charge of fideism—an accusation often directed against Pascal. On the other hand, does a philosophy completely separated from theology and faith not run the risk of setting itself up as a kind of rational tribunal in the face of which theology and faith must present themselves for convalidation and approval?

Framed in these terms, the question seems nearly insoluble. No alternative between theological rationalism and fideism readily appears. But Gilson begs to differ. He argues that there really is an alternative, which is none other than the very thought contained in the writings of Aquinas who, even from a methodological point of view, shows himself much more rigorous and profound than had been thought by those who reproach him for not always sufficiently distinguishing theology from philosophy. In fact, philosophical knowledge is built on interrelated pieces of evidence originally given to us through experience. The light of faith illumines these pieces of evidence, giving them a fundamental hypo-thesis (i.e., an "underlying plan") according to which one can organize both the raw data of human experience and our reflective knowledge of that experience. Knowledge gained in this way is universally human, accessible to everyone from the very beginning. It needs no support of arguments from authority. In fact, if the light of faith actually reveals man's objective, human condition, it can be practically "reconstituted," so to speak, just like when we grope about in a dark room, feeling for the light switch and guided only by the sense of touch. In this sense, philosophy is *ancilla theologiae:* It is an aid to lead us

---

76   See *Studi in onore di G. Bontadini* (Milano: Vita e pensiero, 1975), pp. 454–473. I have especially kept in mind Etienne Gilson. In addition to his classic works *L'esprit de la philosphie médiévale* (Paris: Vrin, 1932) and *La philosophie au moyen age* (Paris: Payot, 1952), see also *Eléménts d'une métaphysique thomiste de l'être* in *Archives d'Histoire Doctrinale et Litterature du Moyen Age,* 48 (1973), pp. 7–36.

along the way of faith, inserting us into the arc of history that is properly and uniquely our own as human beings.

Therefore, as we wrestle with the relationship between philosophy and theology, we must realize that in both cases we are dealing with a wisdom that transcends the alternative between rationalism and fideism, since it does not seek to assent to anything against reason while simultaneously interpreting experience rationally under the light of faith. Its methodological principle is the encounter between faith and experience. It can neither sever itself from faith as rationalism does nor can it place a wedge between faith and human experience as fideism does.

This was precisely Pascal's position. He transcends the opposition between rationalism and fideism. If the immanentist/gnostic position sees continuity from Averroës to Hegel, the Christian position sees continuity stretching from Aquinas to Rosmini down to our own day. It is a continuity based on certain tenets and fundamental texts on the philosophy of God, the philosophy of man, and the relationship between the two. These are then articulated and clarified according to various historical and cultural contexts and different needs arising from scientific progress and similar polemical issues.

We need to make a few final observations about the relevance of Aquinas's philosophy of knowledge for political theory. Naturally, we will have to return to this matter after we have clarified the technical terms used in our discussion. Nevertheless, it would be worth anticipating some of those considerations here. Some of the fundamental categories in the modern philosophy of history and modern political philosophy are essentially influenced by the Averroistic theses on the unicity of the possible intellect —that is, on the existence of a single intellect for the entire human race and a concomitant devaluation of the individual intellect.

The notions of "History" and "State" conceived in the Hegelian tradition—as well as the notion of "Class" developed by Marx—are rooted in Averroës, albeit in different ways.

The self-disclosure of the collective intellect of the species that gives birth to "History" and the "State" is nothing other than a concretization of one particular stage of its development, just as Class arises from a ferment in the negation or as an alternative to the existing situation—the "status quo"—that drives History's never-ending march onward. As the march continues, there is less room for individuality as the individual is deprived of his or her particular rights. Conversely, the fundamental concept of "person"—endowed with intelligence and will—as the locus of responsibility and action, as an essentially free subject of inalienable rights, responsibilities, and duties, cannot be conceived apart from the basis of the intellect's individualization as presented by Aquinas.

General Formulation of the Problem

As I have suggested, from the very beginning philosophy has been fascinated by the paradox of man: He is a finite being who, due to his corporality, belongs to the world of material things, but at the same time is able to stretch toward the infinite. Philosophy has always wrestled with this paradox and tried to take stock of man's natural orientation to the infinite.

The paradox presented by man and his orientation toward the infinite has two fundamental dimensions: a cognitive dimension and a moral dimension. Man, with both his intelligence and his will, is orientated toward the infinite, the ultimate core of what is real—namely, that which is true in itself, beautiful in itself, and good in itself.

These two characteristics—reason and will—essentially and fundamentally distinguish personal being from any other created *ens*. Hence man—a person—is both intelligent and free. Since the time of Plato, philosophy has striven to identify the correct relationship between man's spiritual dimension and material dimension, between his intelligence and free will.[77] This is the context within which we much situate the problem. We might express it in the following way: How is it possible for a finite creature, belonging to the material world, to form rational concepts, universal and abstract, wholly transcendent to matter's potentiality?

This problem finds its first explicit formulation in Socrates and his discovery of the essentially conceptual character of human knowledge. According to Plato's theory, everything that moves in the world has within itself a sufficient principle that causes the specific mode by which it moves. Hence Plato teaches that plants have souls that are in turn the source of

---

77   The case holds even if classical thought tends to identify intelligence and will and equate evil with error rather than sin.

their growth processes. Animals also have souls that account for their vital processes.

Animals possess a certain capacity to form sensible images of the objects with which they come in contact, and they can respond to these images with "feelings" of desire or fear. These "feelings," in turn, motivate reactions of approaching or fleeing. Because of his capacity to know the universal, man is vastly different from lower animals that are limited by an inferior form of knowledge. Man in fact does not simply know what stands in front of him. The sensible image that naturally forms in him, just as it does in other animals, does not merely determine vital reactions in response to a potential threat or a desired good. For man, the sensible image is the starting point of a more complex cognitive process in which *he moves from sensation to concept.* Sensation is the knowledge of things perceived by the senses through direct contact with them. Sensation therefore ceases as soon as the cause provoking it is removed. With the concept, on the other hand, data received through sense perception are unified according to their necessary interrelations. It is difficult to overemphasize the difference between the sensorial image and the concept.[78] Whereas the sensorial image is always particular, the concept is always universal. Sensorial images are interlinked merely through states of consciousness that are conditioned by transformations in the external world. Concepts, on the other hand, are connected to one another through immanent and logically necessary relations. The invention of a concept is therefore the first condition for any scientific elaboration of human thought. The concept derives from sensations through a process of abstraction. From a collection of sensorial images similar to one another, a collection of common data is abstracted, and these common data constitute the fundamental logical structure of all objects belonging to a certain class of things. The role of defining is essential to this process. Through it man attains knowledge not just of the particular in front of him but of the universal.

For example, the universal is directed not toward this determinate neighing animal in front of me but at the equine species with its fundamental and enduring characteristics. Universal knowledge makes it possible to calculate in a rational way the specific behavior of a certain thing and to

78 See for example Plato's *Thaeatetus.*

subjugate the world when knowledge is used for its proper end. But there is another problem: Man does not know universals by reason of the same aspect though which he knows particulars; universals are in fact extracted from sensible knowledge.

On the other hand, the reason by we know universals is not the same as that by which we know particular aspects. Knowing the concept "horse" is not the same as knowing a particular, really existing horse. The difference between knowing a universal and knowing a particular is a sort of paradox: The particular and the universal can never be perfectly superimposed. To the contrary, there can be—and in fact there must be—a discrepancy.

Take the example of geometry. In nature there are many objects that approximate the form of a triangle, but none of them perfectly corresponds to the definition of a triangle. Thus we might think that in order to construct conceptually the form of a real object, we have to use other geometrical forms in addition to the triangle, though these forms are related to the object in different ways. But if this were the case, we would only reach a greater or lesser approximation of the phenomenon to the concept rather than a perfect alignment.

The order of reality is always richer in its determinations than the realm of thought. From this arises a problem: What is the relationship between the concept and the image? In defining the relationship, we will have to recognize above all that the material element necessarily belongs to sensation and not, strictly speaking, to the concept. The material element belongs to sensation in two ways: Sensation makes me aware of a really existing, external thing; the sensation itself is a material modification of the senses, which are corporeal organs.

Conversely, the concept does not refer to any particular material thing but is completely immaterial and spiritual.

What, therefore, is the basis of its existence? Plato imagines that more basic than the material world is an intelligible world where ideas subsist in themselves. The direct experience of objects is an occasion for *recollection*; that is, for remembering the world of ideas that the soul had contemplated before it was immersed in the flesh.[79] Thus the human being has a completely

79   See Plato's *Phaedrus*.

spiritual soul that knows the ideas or forms through a sort of connaturality since it is spiritual and intelligible in itself just as the ideas are.

The Platonic solution runs into two problems: How do material things give rise to the recollection of eternal ideas? How is it possible for an intelligible and spiritual substance like the soul to be united with a body? Who is the real subject of intelligence, man as a whole or simply his soul?

Platonic thought responds to these questions by asserting that between the world of ideas and the world of matter there is a mediator—the Demiurge—who forms the material world after the pattern of the ideas but always in an imperfect way. The form comes to the material from outside. In itself, the form is inchoate and undifferentiated. It follows that there can be no substantial interpenetration between the spiritual soul and the body. In other words, the soul is a prisoner of the body and cannot be united to it substantially.[80]

Aristotle, thoroughly convinced of the substantial unity of the individual human being, adopts a position opposite to that of Plato. For Aristotle the form is not imposed on matter "from the outside." Living beings show us more clearly that the form is the center of the processes of growth and development guided by an innate principle.

We have cognition of the universal not because the particular is an occasion for recollecting the originally contemplated idea but because we are able to engage in a process of abstraction that begins with sensible experience. The form, immanent to the object, is abstracted by the intellect. Aristotle calls the faculty that performs this abstraction the "agent intellect." In sensation the form is "potentially intelligible." By acting upon sensation the agent intellect frees the form and renders it intelligible in act. Once it is rendered intelligible by the agent intellect, the form unites with the receptive faculty of the human soul—the possible intellect—and in that way it effectively becomes known. Human knowledge is something fundamentally

---

80   An excellent general point of reference for Plato is Giovanni Reale, *Platone,* in *Questioni di storiografia filosofica,* ed. V. Mathieu, vol. 1 (Brescia: La Scuola, 1975). See also Francesco Adorno, *Considerazioni conclusive a Platone* (Roma-Bari: Laterza, 1978); Michele Federico Sciacca, *Platone* (Milano: Marzorati, 1967); Adolfo Levi, *Il problema dell-errore nella metafisica e nella gnoseologia di Platone,* ed. Giovanni Reale (Padova: Liviana, 1971).

passive. The possible intellect receives within itself the form that the agent intellect has made intelligible in act. From this we have a fundamental thesis: "*intellegere est quoddam pati.*" Aristotle maintains the human soul's substantial unity. As Plato taught, there are human faculties that correspond to the vegetative soul, the animal soul, and the rational soul, but the human soul is substantially unique and must be thought of as the form of the body and as the principle of its every determination and development.[81]

In Medieval Arabic and Christian thought, Aristotle's position ran into numerous difficulties both on account of problems involved with his own conception of the soul and the difficulties in detaching his conception from the Platonic theses and their successive elaboration in neo-Platonism.

We must ask ourselves: In what exactly does the universal consist as it is known through the process of abstraction? This question, which has to do with Aristotle's logic and psychology, was intensely debated in the thirteenth century and was at the core of the famous disputes concerning the universals.[82]

Two extreme positions immediately sprung up. On one side there were those who refused to abandon the Platonic theory of ideas. These thinkers wanted both the universal—known by the intellect as a definite object with precise, albeit immaterial, consistency and existing apart from the individual and the really existing *ens*—and the human intellect. In the end, in the world of ideas there must be an ideal man—or rather, the idea of man fully realized—and this must also hold true for every concept the human mind is able to formulate. If we abandon this position, argue its supporters, we lose every criterion that allows us to judge what is more and what is less perfect, what is good and what is bad, resulting in total and complete relativism. The other side argues that if we grant these theses, the insoluble problem of the relationship between the idea and reality—especially a living

81 This is the theme of Aristotle's *De anima*. See Franciscus J. Nuyens, *L'evolution de la psychologie de Aristote* (Louvain-La Haye-Paris: Editions de l'Institut Supèrieur de Philosophie, M. Nijohf Uitgevers-Vrin, 1948).

82 On the problem of universals see *Gli universali e la formazione dei concetti,* ed. L. Urbani Ulivi (Milano: Comunità, 1981); Bruno Maioli, *Gli universali. Storia antologica del problema da Socrate al XII secolo* (Roma: Elia, 1970); Rosa Padellaro De Angelis, *Nominalismo e realismo nell'XII secolo;* Mario Dal Pra, *Logica e realtà. Movimenti del pensiero medievale* (Roma-Bari: Laterza, 1974).

reality—immediately arises again, this time with its own autonomous dynamism.

Contrarily, Roscellino de Compiégne opposes the objective existence of the universal. A recent rediscovery of his manuscripts has allowed us to become more familiar with his position, which was previously known only through expositions and critiques by others. Be that as it may, in the history of medieval philosophy his name has remained linked with the thesis that the universal exists uniquely within the human soul. While his main adversary, William of Champeaux, asserted that the universal existed *"ante rem,"* Roscellino placed the universal *"post rem"*—that is, as the result of some simple activity of the intellect. If Plato had taken his starting point from Socrates's discovery of the concept, giving it ontological solidity by means of the theory of ideas (the concept, according to Plato, is nothing other than a reflection within the human being of eternal ideas that have their own ontological stability), Roscellino, in a certain sense, returns to the idea of the concept. The universal is placed entirely within the human faculty of representing the real conceptually.

But we must ask: What exactly corresponds in reality to the concept? What allows us to distinguish true concepts that effectively correspond to the intimate structures of the real, from false concepts that are nothing but a self-illusion of the human spirit? The risk is that the universal will be dissolved into a *"flatus vocis,"* a verbal classification used merely for the sake of convenience as we face the world of nature since it allows us to remember more readily the common characteristics of objects essentially different from and irreducible to one another.

The unity of the intelligible species—that is, of the form that allows us to understand the world—is also in jeopardy; indeed, it falls apart completely.

All these difficulties stem from the incapacity to reconcile two elements that for Aristotle are equally undeniable: the substantial unity of the individual and the composition of matter and form. That is to say that every individual is constituted as an inseparable unity. This unity is the result of two elements that can be isolated conceptually but never exist in reality except by virtue of a reciprocal interdependence. If, the medieval schoolmen asked, they cannot exist except in mutual dependence upon one another, what kind of ontological solidity can we attribute to them when we consider them separately? The problem is quite interesting with regard to universals in general, but in the special and unique case of the human soul it becomes crucial and can only be handled at the level of anthropology.

For Aquinas, the universal has a tripartite existence. First of all, it exists *in re:* The form is immanent to the individual object. This means the intellect abstracts the form and does not create it. This thesis stands as the basis for every epistemological realism; that is, every realistic theory of knowledge.

Secondly, the form is present within the human intellect. Through the process of abstraction, it is received by the possible intellect whenever acted upon by it. The raw, "unprocessed" form becomes an intelligible form by means of the agent intellect's action, and the form then becomes "intellected" insofar as it is taken up by the possible intellect.

All this would be insufficient if, in the end (but actually first of all!), the form were not thought of as existing in the divine intellect. In fact, the species (form) only exists in matter in an "unknowing" way. The material has a form but does not know it has a form. The form, substantially united with matter, is therefore only potentially knowable. If, however, the human intellect is the only place where the form passes from potency into act, then in reality the form exists only in the relationship between object and intellect.

The following question inevitably arises: How does it happen that the potentially intelligible form is found in objects, given that it is really from them that the intellect abstracts the form? If we want to avoid falling into Roscellino's trap, we must admit that the form necessarily exists *ante rem.* Moreover, it exists in God's "intellect" insofar as he creates objects in the world according to that same form. In creating things, God gives them their forms, and the human intellect subsequently abstracts those forms as it comes to know things.

On the other hand, there is neither a world of archetypal ideas nor a Demiurge who shapes matter according to those ideas. Rather, there is an archetypal intellect belonging to God as "person," just as the human intellect belongs to the human person. God forms the ideas and creates things according to those ideas. The solution Aquinas gives to the problem of the universals serves in turn as the general backdrop for the way he confronts the issue of the human soul. Actually, the controversy concerning the human soul recapitulates the same fundamental questions we faced in our analysis of universals, as well as the difficult issue of how we should interpret such questions. Is it possible for the universal to be present in a particular, that is, within the concrete human being? What weight ought we give to the assertion that the universal is *ante rem, in re,* and *post rem*?

A denial that knowledge is the result of the action of an individual subject reappears in Averroës, albeit in a more sophisticated version than in Roscellino or William of Champeaux. Roscellino could not accept the thesis that a particular entity (i.e., man) could know the universal, though he was nonetheless committed to the human character of knowledge. Since he could not admit that human knowledge was capable of attaining universal truth, he had to claim that it was always of only one particular kind, expressed in partial and provisional generalizations and useful solely for classificatory purposes. It is, however, ultimately inadequate for fulfilling the fundamental need to know the essence of things. Things are a bit different with William. He continues to maintain the objective character of knowledge but is forced to ground the objectivity in something outside the realm of human knowledge.

Finally, as noted previously, Aquinas detects within the human intellect a logical capacity for comprehending the universal while simultaneously establishing a relationship between the knowledge of the universal proper to the human person and the knowledge proper to the divine person.

Prior to being in the thing itself, the universal is present first of all in God's knowledge, as God is responsible for creating it, then secondarily in the created thing, and thirdly in the intellect of the knowing subject. Left in these terms, Aquinas's solution is still inadequate and insufficient, for the problem remains: Is the universal that the intellect abstracts from the thing the same universal archetype according to which the thing was first "thought"—and hence created—by God? If we respond with an unconditional "yes" we end up denying, or at least significantly attenuating, the qualitative difference between the human intellect and divine intellect. We come close to the Gnostic thesis of a natural identity between two. Conversely, our analysis has already furnished us with several good reasons for denying a pure identity between the divine intellect and the human intellect. The divine intellect is infinite. The human intellect, in knowing a concept, implies knowledge of each and every real experience of every singular concrete entity falling under any given conceptual category.

In other words, whenever God thinks the concept "man," he simultaneously thinks the entire history of humanity and the individual affairs of every single human being. We, however, who grasp the concept "man" through the process of abstraction, lose our knowledge of the particular whenever we turn to the concept. We can only have knowledge of the particular directly through sense experience, which means in a fragmentary way and in a way proper to us particular, concrete human beings. Our knowledge always refers to those objects that are in the realm of our immediate experience. God's knowledge moves from the universal to the particular. God does not rely on any kind of sense experience, for example, to know what is happening to me at this particular moment; rather, God knows this particular moment as it is included in the idea according to which he created human beings at the beginning of time. For God there is no paradox between the universal and the particular.

For us, however, there is a paradox, and it cannot be eliminated simply by acknowledging the reality of the universal present within the concept.[83] We arrive at knowledge from sense experience, and through the process of abstraction our knowledge is raised to the level of a concept. With the concept, however, comes a loss of the concreteness and historicity of the particular. It is precisely for this reason that the universal in the human intellect lacks the characteristics it has as a universal in the divine intellect. Intellection is a rather feeble attempt to reconstruct an *a posteriori* simulacrum of God's perfect *a priori* knowledge in a fragmentary way. Therein lies the difference between finite and infinite intellects. Between man's intellect—which begins with sense experience—and God's intellect there are angelic intellects. Like the divine intellect, angelic intellects do not begin with sense experience. By knowing themselves and their own spiritual substance they simultaneously enjoy a certain knowledge of the world. In this regard, the angelic intellect resembles the divine intellect: It reaches a particular by departing from the very nature of the idea.[84]

In any case, the range of the angelic intellect is still finite and limited; God's entire creative plan is not present to it (except insofar as God, through grace, elevates the angelic intellect and allows it to contemplate itself).

---

83 Thomas Aquinas, *Quodlibetals*, 10, q. 4, a. 7; *Summa theologiae*, I, q. 16, a. 6; q. 84, a. 4.
84 Thomas Aquinas, *De veritate*, q. 8; *Summa theologiae*, qq. 54, 55, 56, 57, 58.

Moreover, whereas the angelic intellect knows the essence of created things, the *Logos* knows the very genesis of the creative act as internal to the divine substance and Trinitarian love. This observation leads us to consider another characteristic of the divine and infinite intellect that distinguishes it from human and angelic intellects (or at least from separated substances). Namely, the divine intellect is a creative intellect. Its knowledge of things includes the capacity to call them into being—that is, to impart being, reality, or existence to the original ideas. It is a different state of affairs with the finite intellect. The finite intellect cannot draw something from nothingness into being. What it knows is essence, but not with the perfect intuition of the one who endowed it with the gift of being. This is the distinguishing mark of God's *Logos,* or creative word.

The Gnostic philosophical position has always tried to hide or eliminate this difference between the finite and infinite intellects, or at least to confuse the distinction between divine intelligence, angelic intelligence, and human intelligence. We have only to recall the phenomena of magic and alchemy, especially as practiced in the late-medieval and Renaissance periods. They rested on the claim that God's secret, creative word—a word calling things from nothingness into being—was accessible to man. To those initiated through the proper rites, the magic word gave authority over demons and the power to change one element into another.

Above all, the possession of creative wisdom makes man the master and creator of himself. A postage stamp was issued by the German Postal Service for the centenary of Goethe's birth showing an old print of Faust gazing at a homunculus in a test tube, recalling his ambition to build a man using magic and the alchemical forces of nature. Man is finally capable of imitating God's creative energy to the point that he too can create a human being in the same way God did at the beginning of time. But Satan stands in front of Faust, raising a mirror to his face. Gazing at the homunculus, Faust simultaneously sees his own face in the mirror. The symbolic significance is quite profound: Man, in appropriating God's creative power to himself, actually debases himself to the level of a beast, a product made by his own hands. By allowing the devil to minister to him so that he can create a homunculus, Faust ironically has made himself a homunculus in the hands of the devil. That which man pretends to create by imitating God—precisely on account of the natural disproportion between the divine and human intellects—always has an element of imperfection, a defect or a shortcoming. As an angelic intellect tempting man in this way, Satan makes himself a *"simia Dei"* as reflected in the popular saying, "The devil makes the pots but not the lids."[85] Imitation always remains imperfect. A man created by man lacks freedom and love, which cannot be obtained by manipulating matter but only as accepted as a gratuitous gift from God. In a certain sense, modern society can be considered man's colossal attempt to appropriate the infinity of the divine intellect to himself. In making himself the absolute creator of his own destiny and the definer of his own essence, man stoops to the level of a homunculus; he subjects himself to domination. In renouncing his sacred character, man turns himself merely into lump of matter to be used by another man.

The self-alienation and self-destruction that result from man's audacious attempt to take God's place and create a new man—his Promethean aspiration for total self-sufficiency—has inspired a large part of modern literature. This is particularly evident in several characters archetypal of our modern age. Such is the case with Golem, or, in a more romanticized and popular version, Doctor Frankenstein, both of whom are paradigmatic expressions of the unconscious force pervading the current stage of history. The living human being is produced from raw matter by an act of sheer power. But the product ends up being a monster that only destroys itself and others around it.

There is, however, a glimmer of hope: to return to the episode with which we began our analysis, Faust gazes at the homunculus and sees himself in Satan's mirror standing directly at the side of this monstrous creature. Faust's face cannot be eliminated; he is forced to make a choice. Because of his finiteness man is saved from Satan's sin of pride. He is not in a position to distort his God-given face with impunity. Since he is unable to create, the very imperfection of Satan's works means that he is unable to blot out the unique mark of goodness stamped upon the human face; neither can he eliminate the power of human memory that makes man what he is. These are stable and symbolic reference points to which we return again and again. Actually, the devil's temptation is all the more irrational since

---

85   Translator's note: in Italian, "il diavolo fa le pentole ma non i coperchi" is a popular way of saying that the truth will come out in the end.

God has already imparted to man the very creative power he rebelliously strives to usurp. That which the devil's scientist obtains through a life of hard work and research in order to create a human being out of inanimate matter at the cost of his own soul is already within the grasp of every normal human being through the love that unites a man and a woman and enables them to produce offspring. Within the context of a family, human beings have the power to beget human beings physically and spiritually. However, God grants this power to man within a physical, moral, and spiritual order, standing as a reminder that it is only through the memory of being a child, and only through the memory of having once been dependent himself, that he is able to become a creator and a father. Satan's efforts to persuade man to relinquish his own paternity, and to propagate with regard neither for his dependence nor for the affective order of love, are repelled.

There are two aspects to this fundamental acknowledgment of human nature: First, it alerts us to the unique history of each individual, to a father and a mother in the flesh, through whom the individual is connected with the history of man's hopes and disappointments, and becomes an heir of God's promises to Adam to send a Savior. Secondly, human dependence is the dependence of a man upon a woman and a woman upon a man, because only in the love that binds them together is the creation of life truly possible and just. In *Faust*, it is Margarite's love that saves Faust. A woman leads him to discover his humanity.

The preceding considerations have led us a bit astray, but the digression was necessary to emphasize the strong connection between the solution given to the fundamental problem in the metaphysics of knowledge and the complex development of modern culture. Far from being merely the reconstruction of an arcane dispute between some twelfth and thirteenth century sophists, the question of universals lies at the very core of our contemporary problems as it runs through various stages of development leading to our modern culture.

Goethe offers us an example of man's tragic attempt to appropriate the mind and creative power of God. Faust's fate shows us the futility of choosing that path. However, in the more moderate approach of Gnosticism, we see not an attempt to appropriate God's intellect, but an angelic intellect. Perhaps it is in the utter particularity of the angelic intellect that we can reach the heights of divine contemplation. We would then have an intellect that, although unable to create (let alone *self*-create), would nonetheless enjoy the capacity to know reality not from sense experience, but from a direct intellection of essence. This would be a complete knowledge of reality, insofar as the knowledge of general ideas would include the knowledge of all the individual entities that fall under any general idea. In elevating himself to this type of knowledge, man sees things from the same epistemological viewpoint as God. In the history of modern thought, this was precisely the position Leibniz assumed, who believed in the possibility of a deductive knowledge capable of arriving at knowledge of the particular. Indeed, he believed the means to this type of knowledge could be found through the calculation of probability. Pascal, who foreshadowed the same theme from a mathematical perspective, arrived at the opposite conclusion: The human intellect cannot raise itself to the level of the infinite and unconditioned. It is exactly this impossibility that renders the human condition simultaneously noble and tragic in a unique way. If we follow Hegel's line on the matter, we eventually end up holding that man has access to absolute knowledge but that this knowledge necessarily implies a negation of freedom. If it is possible to deduce the entire unfolding of human history and the history of every individual human being simply from the concept "man," then the action of each individual man will be tied to this necessity, and individual freedom will completely disappear. Freedom will be nothing more than the liberty to conform oneself to these necessary occurrences.

Moreover, according to this position, knowledge comes from outside the mediation of sense experience. Hence, there is only one "knowledge" for everyone, since all have the ability to transcend the level of sense experience and assume the viewpoint of the absolute. Since knowledge does not result from individual experience, it will be collective by its very nature. We are dealing with nothing other than the idea of a humanity that together knows and realizes itself in history. Individuals do not elevate themselves to this perspective through abstraction by beginning with the data of sense experience, but rather through negation, distancing themselves from the realm of sense experience.

In all fairness to Hegel, he did take some precautionary measures. Knowledge makes use of intact pieces of sense experience that are already systematized through abstraction. Furthermore, this knowledge comes into play only *post factum*. Historical knowledge of a rational character always follows upon the completion of historical events, and it can neither antic- ipate nor precede those events. But even within these limitations, the Hegelian system substantially transposes the mechanism of angelic intelli- gence and raises it to the level of common intelligence. Nevertheless, it is always an angelic intelligence of a particular type—it knows the totality and adds that totality to itself, transcending individual empirical intelli- gences, a sort of collective intellect of the species.

A consequence of the Faustian identification of the divine intellect with the individual human intellect by means of imitation is the specification of an angelic intellect as the sole intellect of the whole human race. Another consequence of Hegel's identification is the denial of a difference between angelic intellects and the divine intellect. In conformity with his funda- mental neo-Platonic/Gnostic inspiration, Hegel considers the angelic in- tellect as one moment in the articulation of the divine process of knowledge/creation of the world. Nevertheless, with regard to the universal, which is always present—albeit in different ways—in man, in the world, and in God, the gnostic position contradicts the substantial unicity of the universal and its mode of being. Hence, since the time of Averroës, this po- sition is made possible on the basis of an opinion about the human soul rather than a doctrine of universals.

2. Averroës and Aquinas

Even though the Gnostic doctrine of universals had already been rejected, we find a resurgence of Gnosticism in Averroës, but this time with a twist.[86]

---

86   On Averroës, see Goffredo Quadri, *La filosofia araba nel suo fiore*, in 2 volumes (Florence: La Nuova Italia, 1939); the introduction to Saint Thomas by Bruno Nardi entitled *Trattato sull'unità dell'intelletto contro gli averroisti* (Firenze: San- soni, 1947); Fernand van Steenberghen, *Aristotle in the West* (Louvain: Nauwe- laerts, 1955) and *La philosohie au XIII siècle* (Louvain-Paris: Bèatrice Nauwelarts, 1966); Salvador Gomez Nogales, *Filosofia musulmana y human- ismo integral de Santo Tomàs*, Miscelánea Camillas, 47–48 (1967), pp. 229– 265; Ludwig Hödl, "*Über dei averroistische Wende der lateinischen Philosophie des Mittelalters im 13. Jahrhundert*," *Rechershces de théologie ancienne et médié- vale*, 39 (1972), pp. 171–204. There is no work more pertinent to the question that interests us here than that of Bernhard Bürke on Averroës's commentary

The question is no longer whether the universal is *ante rem, post rem,* or *in re.* It is now whether the human soul, as the locus of the universal, can be considered something qualitatively different from the angelic intellect—or, better yet, from the divine intellect.

According to Averroës, human knowledge is already engaged in sense experience when the sense organs are impressed by the phantasm—the sensorial image—of the object. The phantasm then undergoes an initial systemization by the passive intellect, which arranges the sensorial data into a unified structure.[87] At this point the agent intellect intervenes, abstracting from sensible matter the *species* (i.e., the universal) that was already intelligible in potency but now rendered intelligible in act. Finally, the intelligible species in act enters a relation with the possible intellect by modifying it so that it becomes known in act. Hence, this sequence is exactly the same as Aristotle's but with a fundamental twist: The agent intellect and the possible intellect are not two faculties proper to the intellect of the individual, but two real meta-individual potencies with the character of separated substances rather than a single human soul. This is therefore a position that denies any commingling between the sensible and the intelligible and views the soul as a form strictly tied to the body, but at the same time as a spiritual element foreign to the body and entrapped or imprisoned within it. This spiritual element, qualitatively equal in all men, is also, according to Averroës, the same for the whole

on Aristotle's Metaphysics. See *Das neunte Buch des lateinischen grossen Mataphysik-Kommentars von Averroës. Text-Edition und Vergleich mit Albert dem Grossen und Thomas von Aquin* (Berlin: Francke Verlag, 1969). For a summary, see Léon Gauthier, *Ibn Roschd (Averroès)* (Paris: Presses Universitaires de France, 1948).

87 The notion of passive intellect, widely disseminated in the Middle Ages thanks to Aquinas, is generally not accepted by modern scholars. In the third book of his *De Anima,* Aristotle explains in chapter 4 that the possible intellect is incorruptible and separable, while in chapter 5 he explains that the passive intellect is corruptible. The medieval commentators tried to reconcile this contradiction in Aristotle by developing an autonomous concept of passive intellect as the material support for the spiritual action of the intellect. This is the root of the Averroist crisis. See Thomas Aquinas, *Sententia libri De anima,* 3, lect. 10, 745. For Averroës, the passive intellect stands at the apex of the individual human's participation in the knowing process.

human race.[88] In fact, if the possible intellect is the place where the ideas of all things are preserved, and if these ideas are qualitatively identical to one another, it follows that all possible intellects are identical with one another. But this can only be possible if there are material beings identical among themselves and not sharing the same act of existence. They remain distinct from one another in matter, space, and time. If we think of the soul as being entirely of a "conceptual" nature, the factors of matter, space, and time are of no consequence. "Identical" intellects are in fact the same intellect.[89] Thus the human intellect remains one even though it possesses many forms and operates at a variety of cognitive levels. A better or worse ordering of the sensible material supplied to the passive intellect results in greater or lesser development of the self-knowledge attained by the passive intellect in individual empirical subjects.

But how is it possible to reconcile these positions with empirical experience that clearly points to the individual character of knowledge? How is it possible to hold that there is a single possible intellect in all men with the cognitive act of an individual man? Averroës develops a theory of the possible intellect's continuation and participation in the knowing subject though the phantasms of the passive intellect. Since the phantasm remains the point of departure for the cognitive act, and since the phantasm is different in different human subjects, it follows that the act itself is different and leads to a different modification of the possible intellect as it receives into itself the intelligible species abstracted from particular phantasms. Moreover, for Averroës, the individualization of the cognitive act occurs not only through a diversity of particular experiences reflected in the diversity of phantasms, but also through a diversity of knowing subjects insofar as the phantasm is prepared for the abstracting action of the agent intellect by the faculties of imagining, remembering, and thinking, through which the sense impressions receive their initial structuring. Different sensations can in fact be remembered and compared to one another.

---

88 Cf. Averroës *Long Commentary on the De Anima,* comm. 4–8 and 36. Unlike the problem of the unity of the agent intellect, Averroës is virtually the only major medieval commentator who takes this view. He nonetheless does so with a high level of coherence.

89 *Ibid.* comm. 5.

Memory is not unique to man. It is a property of higher animals, and the same could be said of imagination. But this does not hold in the case of a *virtus cogitativa*—that is, the capacity to take apart and reassemble sensorial experience in its elementary components. Here we are closer to the realm of the intellect, and it is indeed the faculty that Aristotle properly calls the passive intellect. The effective functioning of the agent intellect depends on the effective functioning of the passive intellect, insofar as the latter brings together the material of experience. The greater the capacity of the *virtus cogitativa* to break down sensible experience by isolating the analogous elements of complex experiences and connecting them to one another, the more easily and effectively follows the action of the agent intellect.

The diversity of concrete experiences and the diversity of the passive intellect's operation work together to individualize each cognitive act. The passive intellect is the point of contact between the knowing individual and the possible intellect. By means of a union between the passive and possible intellects, brought about through a single knowing act, the knowing individual is in a position to participate in knowledge of the universal. The possible intellect is made present to the individual through its forms, which constitute the intelligible species, forms it deduces in turn from its contact with the phantasm contained within it. We can therefore describe the passive intellect as the touchstone by which the possible intellect, a type of intelligence unaware of itself, is drawn to knowledge of itself through contact with the phantasm that comes to it from the sensible world.

This is the thrust of Aquinas's critique.[90] His reasoning unfolds entirely on par with Aristotle's doctrine of the soul, and it is on that level that we will initially follow it. Then we will see if it is possible to draw some general conclusions. On the surface, the dispute seems to revolve around the way the cognitive act is brought to completion. But in reality it implies an entirely different way of comprehending knowledge and consequently an entirely different anthropology.

---

90   See *Scriptum super Sententias*, 2, d. 17, q. 2, a. 1; *Summa contra gentiles*, 2, cc. 59, 73, 75; *Summa theologiae*, I, q. 76, a. 1–2; *Sententia libri De anima*, 3, lects. 7 and 8, and all of the *De unitate intellectus*, particularly cc. 4 and 5; *Compendium theologiae*, 85; *De spiritualibus creaturis*, a. 9.

It is easy to discern two fundamental principles in Aquinas that are continually referred to throughout his discussion: the reality of the human soul and its indissoluble "informing" of the human body. That which makes man "man," and that which gives him his specific form, is his capacity to know the universal. To take this away from the individual means nothing less than to take away that which makes him an individual. It is easy to see how Aquinas's position on this matter is intimately tied to his metaphysics of knowledge, as well as the fundamentally personalist inspiration of his ethics and political philosophy. All of this can be considered as derivative of and corollary to the fundamental Thomistic thesis that "the soul is a spiritual substance united to the physical body as its form."[91] This is what the *mysterium hominis* consists in. The union is so immediate that the soul is the act of the body, or its very existence as a specifically human body. Hence there is no need to place an intermediate term between the body and the soul to complete their unity. The entire anti-Averroist argument, as we shall see, is a development and defense of this thesis.[92] First and foremost, Aquinas employs an argument that directly refers to the fundamental thesis we alluded to earlier—namely, it is not possible for the presence of a phantasm to constitute man as an intelligent being. In fact, prior to its being acted upon by the abstracting power of the agent intellect, the phantasm is only potentially intelligible. If, therefore, the possible intellect is made present within the individual only be means of the phantasm, it is in fact not actually present in the individual at all.[93]

91   *Summa contra gentiles*, 2, c. 68.
92   It is interesting to note that the principle axis around which Aquinas's argument against the Averroists turns is not anti-naturalist or a defense of Platonic elements against naturalistic Aristotelian elements. It is rather a defense of the Aristotelian revolt, motivated by a neo-Platonic sensibility, against the refusal to admit the possibility of a union between a spiritual substance and a physical body as form and matter. This is especially clear in the way Aquinas argues in the *Summa contra gentiles*. The anti-Averroistic argument unfolds in book 2, chapter 56 *(per quem modum substantia intellectualis possit corpori uniri)* to book 2, chapter 90 *(Quod nulli alii corpori nisi humano unitur substantia intellectualis ut forma)*.
93   See *Summa contra gentiles*, II, c. 73: "*Secundum enim dictam positionem, nihil ad intellectum pertinens remanebit numeratum secundum multitudinem hominum, nisi solum phantasma; et hoc ipsum phantasma non erit numeratum*

In short, it must be one or the other. Either the intelligible species is present in the human intellect's act (and hence the faculty of grasping the universal concept proper to the possible intellect must be attributed to the human intellect), or it is not, in which case man lacks the peculiar quality that makes him a *person*—that is, an intelligent and free being. In the latter case, man would be demoted to the level of sensitive animals that have sense impressions completely analogous to the phantasms in man. Averroës's objection that the human passive intellect nevertheless *still* belongs to the single individual is invalid.[94] Indeed, it is true that the *virtus cogitativa* distinguishes man from other animals. This power, however, does not make him an intelligent and free being but merely an animal more perfect than other animals. The *virtus cogitativa* does not regard the universal, rather the particulars. That is, it pertains to the content of experience organized according to pseudo-concepts (to borrow a term of Benedetto Croce) that do not touch upon the universal and do not themselves have any claim to truth. The work of the *virtus cogitativa* may be considered a precursor to the action of the agent intellect, in which case it is placed within the context of man's general spiritual activity. However, it can also be detached from its connection to the soul's higher faculties directed at the knowledge of truth. In this scenario, we have what Augustine called a *scientia inordinata*, which modern critical sociology refers to as "instrumental reason." That is, it is reason which breaks down and reassembles material gathered from experience—not for the purpose of discovering truth but for actualizing man's power over things, including other men. Man is consequently the most

> *secundum quod intellectum est in actu, quia sic est in intellectu possibili et est abstractum a materialibus conditionibus per intellectum agentem. Phantasma autem, secundum quod intellectum est in potentia, non excedit gradum animae sensitivae."*
>
> In fact, according to Aquinas's position, if there is a plurality of persons, then nothing regarding the intellect would remain distinct if not the phantasm (the sense impression). And the phantasm itself would not be distinct as intellected in act, since in this form it subsists in the possible intellect and is abstracted according to the material conditions by the work of the agent intellect. Conversely, insofar as it remains intellected only in potency, the phantasm does not exceed the level of the sensitive soul.

94 Cf. *Summa contra gentiles*, 2, c. 60.

magnificent and awe-inspiring animal in the entire cosmos. In reality, however, the knowledge most proper to man—that which makes him what he
is—is his knowledge of the transcendental categories of the true, the beautiful, the good, and the one. It is these that form man's intellectual, ethical,
aesthetic, and religious life. It is also in light of these that the power of tech-
nology might be directed to properly human ends.

A disciple of Averroës might nonetheless claim that his position does
not deny the presence of the good, the beautiful, the true, and the one
within the history of human culture. He simply denies that such ideas are
immanently present within the intellect of the individual man. He attributes them to the common intellect of humanity. In this way, the individual
is inevitably debased to the status of a higher animal exploited for the purpose of actualizing a truth that does not directly interest him. Hence the
good as realized in history cannot be *the good of the person* but only the
good of an entirely different order to which man must submit himself by
denying his corporeality and interests, including the values indelibly impressed upon his soul. This is what happens in Hegelian philosophy:
Through the higher wisdom of *Geist*, the individual, in pursuing his particular ends, actually serves the comprehensive plan of the Universal. But
while this philosophy might posit an unequivocal continuity between the
particular and the universal by making the particular a support—or rather
an occasion for—the realization of the universal, it actually opens up an
unbridgeable gap between them. It is not without reason that one of the
greatest problems in all idealistic philosophy is that of passing from the
Ideas (the universal) to Reality (the particular)—or rather of reconciling
the universal and the particular. In the end, this reconciliation will not be
realized through an analysis of the effective experience of the really existing
man; rather—by a wave of the magic wand of philosophy—it must be pos-
tulated as the necessary and revolutionary result of history.

As we have already alluded to in our review of the polemic between
Aquinas and Averroës, it is not simply a question of the modality of knowledge but of the type of knowledge. The Averroist claims that the universal
recomposed within the possible intellect is not the abstracted conceptual
universal as understood by the Aristotelian tradition, but rather a concrete
universal, so to speak. By putting together the individual intellective acts
of all existing men throughout history it is possible to construct a universal

that not only brings together formal and abstract characteristics but also constitutes the concrete process of becoming in history. Hence God's entire creative project in its historical unfolding is reflected *post factum* in the possible intellect. The possible intellect actualizes the human spirit's knowledge of itself.[95] On the other hand, since man is endowed with knowledge and is himself a certain microcosmic reflection of the entire cosmos, then the human spirit, through its own self-knowledge, attains the knowledge of all created realities. This knowledge exists in three ways: *ante rem* (as a pure idea in the creative spirit of God), *in re* (in created nature), and *post rem* (in the human intellect). Thus we can say that the human spirit participates in the divine substance's process of development and self-knowledge. Here we encounter the *exitus/reditus* rhythm characteristic of Gnosticism. The divine substance comes out of itself by lowering itself through the creation of the world and returning to itself in the human spirit.[96]

If we pause to examine the kind of humanity implied by this schema, we face a conflicted and contradictory notion of personhood. There is no certainty about how the life of the individual person develops and what ethical choices we can attribute to him. It is a philosophy that fuels a fascination with history and the becoming of the totality. Averroës's method inevitably leads toward the impossibility of constructing a true and meaningful ethical system. Since the intelligent soul is not really joined to the body as its form, it follows that what pertains to the body does not necessarily pertain to the soul and *vice versa*. The relationship to the totality does not pass through an individual's finite acts and his autonomous assumption of responsibility within the world; rather, it occurs when a person keeps himself and his finite individuality at a safe distance from events. This distancing can take different forms. It can lead to a depreciation of the body and its inherent rights, a denial of the passions and, and ultimately a denial of essential bodily needs by practicing vicious asceticism. This is the way of

95 Aquinas continually returns to this point. If it is a separated substance, the possible intellect acquires its knowledge directly from separated substances and not from experience, and the model of angelic knowledge substitutes that of human knowledge.

96 This same triadic rhythm is found in the Hegelian system. See the studies of Della Volpe in *Hegel romantico e mistico,* and of Bloch in *Avicenna und di aristotelische Linke,* both cited above.

gnosis, a rigorism that can lead, for example, to the repudiation of marriage. Moreover, it can lead to us to believe that an individual's behavior is utterly irrelevant to his salvation, which in turn unleashes a complete legitimization of immorality. Essentially, a certain forgetfulness of one's body can be attained through pleasure in a way analogous to extreme asceticism. This is the sensualistic tendency of *gnosis.*

Both situations undermine the Catholic teaching on marriage and its claim that the body and human sexuality are *loci* for expressing the soul's substantial values and are not to be rejected as burdensome (either through indulgence or repression) for the sake of some "higher" contemplation. When, therefore (as in a modern form of *gnosis*) the universal is understood in purely historical terms, another solution to the problem emerges— namely, the appropriation and absorption of the private realm into the political realm, since political action alone has the capacity to join the individual to the universal as it is actualized through history.[97]

In this way, ethics is engulfed by politics. The supreme good is divested of its ethical character. The person's real perfection and the fulfillment of his unique identity are not brought about through any relation to a universal. To the contrary, the greatest good is realized through a total, unmitigated adherence to the universal, accompanied by a complete dismissal of one's own life and particular destiny (which are illusory), thus eviscerating ethics of its importance as the systematic actualization of the good in one's own life. Ethics is replaced by *gnosis:* knowledge by initiation into a way that leads to self-abnegation and union with *the* Universal.

To counter this idea, Aquinas presents an alternative view of how we attain knowledge of the mode of the universal's presence in the human intellect. For Aquinas, the universal can come to exist in the human subject only through a process of abstraction. This process occurs uniquely for each individual person, each having distinct access to the truth, even if inchoate and partial. Our knowledge of things remains external. If the Universal totally manifested itself in history, then knowledge of history would amount to knowledge of God.

---

97   See Livio Sichirollo, *"Dialettica e Politica in Aristotele," Bollettino di storia della filosofia,* 2 (1974), pp. 102–123*)," Rivista critica di storia della filosofia,* 31 (1976), pp. 164–192; Patrick De Laubier, *"Sociologie d'Aristote et de Marx," Revue Thomiste,* 76 (1976), pp. 34–58.

In the form I have described it so far, Aquinas's argumentation against the thesis of a single possible intellect simply notes the antinomy toward which the Averroistic position tends as it attempts to confront the problem of the species. Through a sort of paradoxical reasoning that radically proposes a possible opposition between sensible knowledge and intelligible knowledge, attributing a different species of soul to each, Averroës ends up obfuscating the distinction between the sensible and the intelligible—that is, the difference between the species and the phantasm. To better grasp Aquinas's argument in its entirety, we must look at how he unmasks the irrelevance of the concrete individual arguments that favor the unity of the possible intellect. Only then will we have a better understanding of his reformulation of Aristotle's theory of knowledge.

As we have seen, a key difficulty sparking the Averroistic position is the problem of the apparent impossibility of the possible intellect's individuation. This is what leads Averroës to postulate its unity. In fact, separate substances, insofar as they are intellectual substances, are distinguished from one another only through the species. In the case of corporeal beings, the difference demarcating one being from another within the same species is corporeality, by quantitatively diverse material that sets off one thing from another. In this way, one form—"dog," for example—is materially individuated in the millions of beings that belong to the species "canine." This obviously does not hold for separated forms or "ideas." Devoid of matter, a separated form can only be identified by its internal conceptual determination—that is, by its form. In the case of separated substances, a plurality of individuals belonging to the same species is inconceivable. Every separated substance constitutes a unique species. Stated in these terms, the problem inevitably forces us to confront an either-or situation: Either the possible intellect is individuated by matter (which would seem to contradict its conceptual and spiritual character), or it must necessarily be conceived as entirely unique for each and every human being (given that it would be impossible to distinguish an internal and immaterial difference of one man's possible intellect from another's).[98]

Conversely, if we allow for a plurality of possible intellects, we are forced to admit that the intelligible species of things is present in each of them. But

98 Thomas Aquinas, *De spiritualibus creaturis,* a. 9 ad. 2, 3, 4.

the species, which is universal, is one. It cannot be otherwise. So how is it possible to preserve the universality of knowledge if we allow a plurality of particular intellects? Do we not risk having to admit that every single intellect constitutes its own complete cognition with its own particular intelligible species, in a way that makes it completely autonomous from other intellects? This would result in a kind of anarchy of knowledge, an absolute domination of opinion and the end to science. Ultimately, the unity of knowledge is the last target of the Averroistic revolution.[99] If we admit a plurality of possible intellects—i.e., one for each member of the human species—all of which contain the same knowledge, we would have to explain how each of these individual subjects has the capacity to possess the same item of knowledge, each in his own unique way and individualized from the intelligible species found in his possible intellect. In order to postulate a plurality of *cognitiones,* all of which are identical to one another by virtue of their form, we would have to imagine a single form of cognition individualized by different material instances. By definition, however, this is impossible due to the immaterial character of knowledge. Thus, although there are good reasons to discard the thesis of the possible intellect's unity, there are equally good reasons to reject the theory of a plurality of possible intellects.

Aquinas responds to these objections by drawing on fundamental principles regarding the nature of the soul, against which Averroës's argument is primarily directed. The soul is a spiritual substance united to a physical body as its form. Indeed, this presents a paradox that Averroës is unwilling to accept. As a spiritual substance, the soul has its own *esse intellegibile* distinct from the being of the body. However, by virtue of the soul's unity, as the form of the body its intelligible and autonomous *esse* is irreversibly adapted to be the form of a determinate body. Let us not forget the soul's essential characteristics: as a spiritual substance it has the capacity to grasp the universal and the infinite.

---

99   Averroës, *Long Commentary on the De Anima,* comm. 5. If there is no unity of the possible intellect, "it will be impossible for the pupil to learn from the master, unless the knowledge of the master is a power that creates and generates knowledge within the pupil, in the way that a fire generates another fire which is similar to it regarding the species. Such a thing, however, is impossible."

This capacity, however, remains in a state of pure potency. Unlike separated substances, the human soul has no content of its own; it can only apprehend things through the mediation of the body's sense experience and by abstracting from that experience.

The soul has its own unique way of reaching the universal by starting from a determined complex of historical experience. If every spiritual substance can be distinguished from others based on the unique collection of knowledge constituted by its own self-consciousness, then analogously we may say that the soul can be defined in terms of its consciousness of a certain unique complex of human experience. Just as separated substances, starting from a consideration of the concept of what they are in themselves, are differentiated by knowing an identical reality and identical concepts "analytically," so to speak, so the human soul attains knowledge of the universal by starting with a reflection on the individual experience defining its origin, context, and means of knowing.

Thus if the soul is joined to the body as its form, and if the soul is a unity in itself, it follows that the intellectual parts of the sous—i.e., those parts that correspond to the conceptual faculties and make man to be what he is, even when they are not directly individualized by matter—will nonetheless be individualized by the body to which they belong and which allows them to have the experience that serves as the basis for all knowledge.

Aquinas counters Averroës's second objection by noting that the Arabic philosopher ignores a fundamental distinction between *id quod intelligitur* and *id quo intelligitur*—that is, between the object known and the means of knowledge. The species is not the object of knowledge; it is its instrument. The object of knowledge is the really existing thing external to the human soul; or better yet, the proper object of knowledge is the *ratio*, the rational and universal core that is the formal cause of things and determines them to be precisely what they are. "*Id vero quod intelligitur est ipsa ratio rerum existentium extra animam.*"[100] To know the universal is to know the immanent *ratio* of things. This is to say that the species should not be thought of in a neo-Platonic way as conceived by Averroës—that is, as an "intellectual being" buried within things and uncovered only through the knowing act.

100 *Summa contra gentiles*, 2, c. 76.

The species is in fact the universal as it exists in the human intellect; that is, as it is apprehended in a human way. But this is radically differentiated from the universal's way of existing in the object. *"Quamvis enim ad veritatem cognitionis necesse sit ut cognitio rei respondeat, non tamen oportet quod idem sit modus cognitionis et rei."*[101] In the thing, the universal exists as individuated by matter and as the form of matter, from which it is abstracted by the intellect in the act of knowing. The unity of the universal rests solidly on its immanent presence within the object (i.e., the being toward which knowledge is ultimately directed).

In this way, Aquinas avoids Averroës's trap. If the universal is one, either we must say that it subsists in itself, independent of the human cognitive act in a way similar to the Platonic ideas (which would be a return to William of Champeaux's position), or we must posit a single knowing subject as the foundation of the universal's unity (which is precisely what Averroës does). For Aquinas, the basis for the unity of the universal is found in the being's *ratio* and form, from which the species is abstracted. Just as there is no contradiction in a plurality of complex images all found within a single object, neither would there be any contradiction in a single form having a plurality of intelligible species, as is clearly evident through the various sensible experiences of diverse individual intellects. Nevertheless, the universal does not subsist outside the human spirit *per se;* as the latter comes to know the former, the intellect intends something external to the human soul. On the basis of this principle, it seems rather easy to respond to the third difficulty advanced by the Averroists: knowledge is unified for all those possessing it because the object to which their intellective act turns is a unity. At the same time, insofar as the intellective act, oriented toward the same object by several different subjects, is individual in itself, knowledge is not "one" but diverse. By means of the species formed by the intellect—in which the material foundation for the universality of thought (i.e., the unity of the forms of things known) is clearly apparent—the individual knower appropriates to himself a single "knowledge" (i.e., *scientia*); from this perspective, nothing impedes *scientia* from existing in several different knowing subjects provided the material identity of its content remains intact. The tension between Aquinas and Averroës touches on a central question in

101 *Ibid.*

modern philosophy—namely, the so-called problem of providing grounds for affirming the reality of the external world; or, as it is more generally called, the problem of idealism.

There is a particular kind of popular idealistic philosophy according to which the reality of the external world is denied the materiality it seems to have in our sense experience in order to assert the sole reality of the "idea." Now that we have examined Averroës's formulation of the problem of knowledge, we are in a better position to understand the idealist problem. Idealism does not necessarily deny that sensation is the point of departure for the cognitive process. It simply stresses, with good reason, that sensation is not yet a concept, and that the concept contains more "truth" than "sensation." The concept, in fact, concerns the universal, whereas sensation regards merely the particular. At this point, however, if the universal coincides unilaterally with the *species intelligibilis*, then the basis for the universal character of knowledge will be entirely internal to the cognitive act.

According to the Averroistic point of view, it is the knowing subject, through the intellect's organizing activity, that confers universality and establishes a sure rational connection to the real, which, in itself, is only a disordered collection of sense impressions.[102] The species is not the human intellect's reflection of the *ratio* immanently present in created things. Rather, it is the *ratio* projected onto the real world by the possible intellect so that the mind can arrange its experience into some kind of order. This is the seminal idea that gave birth to idealism. Idealism does not deny the reality of the external world and the sensorial basis of all experience. It rather attributes the formation of ideas and the "moment" of our discovery of the universal exclusively to the activity of the knowing subject.

102 This would appear to be similar to a transcendentalist reading of the Averroistic position. If the possible intellect, which contains the species, does not derive from the experience of the individual subject, the comprehension of the particular reality according to universal categories will have to be thought necessarily as the effect of the projection of the species by the transcendental "I" (i.e., a separated possible intellect) upon the unordered plurality of sensible data. Here we are close to Kant's position in the *Critique of Pure Reason*. There seems to be an analogy between this and the fundamental approach of Karl Rahner in his *Geist in Welt*. See Thomas Aquinas, *Summa contra gentiles*, 2, c. 73.

In this regard, the Averroistic position on intelligible species is a direct prelude to Kant. In Kant we also have the complete acknowledgement of the external world's reality, though it attributes the production of the universal—which is the only true and proper object of knowledge—to the activity of the subject. Indeed, Averroës's position is much more radically idealistic than Kant's. Kant avoids the complete overlapping of the *id quod intelligitur* with the *id quo intelligitur* by conceding that something of the object toward which the knowing act is directed escapes the power of comprehension. This "something" also happens to be the most essential nucleus: the *noumen*. In the face of this intelligible order established by the intellect through its own activity stands another possible order, potentially more objective, but nevertheless unknowable. Averroës goes much further in identifying the idea with the real: The species produced by the intellect is that which is known, as well as that which grounds the universality of knowledge.

These considerations also clarify the inseparable link that connects idealist epistemology to, on the one hand, the affirmation of the unicity of the human intellect, and, on the other hand, the realist epistemological position that maintains a plurality of individual intellects. If, in fact, the foundation for universality is placed within the subject, it is impossible to preserve the unity of human knowledge and therefore to preserve the universal validity of ideas and inter-subjective communication, without at the same time conceding the unity of the cognitive act for the whole human race that grounds its universality. Realists find themselves in the opposite situation. Precisely because they ground the universality of the cognitive act in the thing, they can allow for multiple individual intellects without sacrificing either the principle of inter-subjective communication or the universality of knowledge. The foundation of both consists precisely in the recognition that the basis of universality—i.e., that which is intended in the concept—is the *ratio* immanently present in the thing. It is not hard to see the theological consequences of this.

In the way described thus far, the cognitive act is explained essentially in terms of receptivity with respect to the truth contained within the thing, thus requiring a disposition of "attentiveness" and "dependence" on the part of the knower.

Furthermore, recognizing the *ratio*'s immanence in the object necessarily gives rise to the question of its origin—i.e., the principle of its presence within the object. This brings us back to God's creative presence in the world, who gives the thing its being and essence. The ethical attitude implied by the Averroistic position is quite different. Here, the cognitive act is not fundamentally receptive and contemplative. It rather posits man as the one who imparts form to the chaotic mix of multiple sense impressions that bombard him. Moreover, he considers his own spirit to be the source of the rational order appearing in the world of nature, and will even attempt to confer material existence to this order by subjecting it to his dominion. The phenomenon of revolution is nothing other than the transference of this cognitive attitude to the practical realm: The real, which has no binding *ratio* for the knower, is merely a kind of prime matter receiving its form from man himself. However, if understood correctly, the idea of the human intellect's creative activity with respect to reality is not entirely foreign to Thomistic philosophy. According to Aquinas, man "manipulates" the real but always with respect to the *ratio* immanently present within it. For Averroës, this manipulation occurs apart from any external guiding law. The natural law, discoverable by the intellect, does not have to be respected but rather utilized so that man may exercise control over the real. In the end, the criterion for truth does not consist in a strict correspondence between the *ratio* and the thing, but rather in a kind of internal coherence, and therefore only in a theoretical plausibility.

In order to affirm man's substantial unity and his capacity to know the truth, and in order to verify the scholastic axiom according to which man is an intelligent and free being whose intelligence and freedom are the reason for his likeness to God, we cannot simply dismiss the Averroistic thesis about the unity of the possible intellect.

In fact, an even more potent challenge to Christian thought is the seemingly more moderate position of Avicenna which, while recognizing the plurality of the possible intellect, maintains the unicity of the agent intellect.[103] This thesis was particularly attractive to the medieval mindset

---

103 See Aristotle, *De anima*, c. 5; Avicenna, *De Anima*, bk. 5, c. 5 and *Metaphysica*, bk. 9, c. 3; Averroës *Long Commentary on the De Anima*, comm. 17–20; Thomas Aquinas, *In II Sent.*, d. 17, q. 2, a. 1; *De Veritate*, 10, 6; *Summa contra gentiles*, cc. 76–78; *Summa Theologiae*, I, q. 79, a. 4, e5; *De Anima*, 3, lect. 10; *Compendium Theologiae*, 86; *De spiritualibus creaturis*, a. 10.

insofar as it incorporated aspects reminiscent of Augustine's notion of the *lumen*. According to Augustine, the grace that comes from God in the Word, and which is the Word itself, is the light that illuminates all things and enables us to know the truth. What could have possibly been more plain to the medieval mindset, still accustomed as it was to rigorous distinctions between different levels of thought, than to make Avicenna's agent intellect coincide with Augustine's *lumen* and then to transpose the Augustinian theory of our knowledge of the divine mystery through grace to a theoretical understanding of our knowledge of the world? This transference was made all the more easily since, as previously noted, Avicenna's pages were filled with a powerful mystical spirit.[104] However, his is a pantheistic and Gnostic mysticism foreign to Christian understanding. By transposing the Augustinian theory of *lumen* to Avicenna's theory of the unity of the agent intellect, we risk short-circuiting the necessary distinction between nature and faith. Although such a transposition initially seems to offer a Christian solution to the problem presented by the rise of new forms of scientific thought and by placing them at the center of the Christian worldview, in reality it undermines the historical dimension of a radically new and particular knowledge of God made possible through the revelation of Christ, and renders it a special case within the normal means available to man to make sense of reality. In this vein, we also have to recall another element of Avicenna's teaching: The religious spirit of his thought is totally concentrated on the One. Although some aspects of his work incited the hostility of theologians who were firmly committed to the letter of orthodox Islamic law, it is undeniable that Avicenna was a thinker entirely within the logic and spirit of Islam.

From a philosophical point of view, Islam is the most logically elaborated form of monotheism. It is the completion, so to speak, of Hebrew monotheism after its renunciation of the doctrine of the Trinity. Historical Judaism denies this development by opting for a literal fidelity to the tradition, eschewing any possibility of further development. This development is thus present in the course of world history through Islam. Islam rejected the Christian doctrine of the Trinity because it seemed self-contradictory.

104 William of Auvergne and Roger Bacon agree with this position, as do many other Augustinians.

At the same time, at least in its orthodox formulation, Islam fails to recognize that monotheism itself seems contradictory. For the strict monotheistic rigorist, God only is, and it is not possible for anything else to exist in addition to him or alongside him. If in fact God is One while simultaneously existing as the "whole," then nothing can exist outside of God as the One. Everything that exists will have to be reduced to the One not simply as the source of its being, but also as the primordial determination of its being. The One is in all things, and all things are in the One. As soon as we detect any tension between the individual and Infinite Being, we must somehow resolve it by framing the existence of everything into the One. This can easily lead to a rejection of every limited determination of finite being, including man. This has clear anthropological implications: The real is recapitulated in man who himself is dissolved in the One.[105] This is precisely the vision of the Trinity precluded by the Catholic worldview. The Catholic vision permits us to think of the One as a community of persons in which men and women can be inserted through the fruits of redemption without in any way renouncing their individual personalities. The notion of the Trinity is at the very heart of this dialectic. It contains the very possibility of surpassing finite subjectivity by preserving and esteeming it. Apart from this Trinitarian perspective (which naturally includes the Incarnation of the Word), the individual intellect is absorbed into the One, and the whole theory of angelic substances is a way to resolve this absorption.

These considerations once again show how superficial and mundane it is to reduce the thirteenth-century dispute between Avicennism/Averroism and Thomism to a controversy between the scientific spirit offered by the Aristotelian works on natural philosophy and religious obscurantism. It is a dispute that, in a certain way, simply recognizes the validity of Aristotelian thought in its own context. The situation is, of course, much more complex. If, on the one hand, Aristotelian thought is truly open, unresolved in itself, and open to being expanded in more than one direction, then it is also true that Christianity is not so much threatened by Aristotelian naturalism as it

---

105 We will encounter this mysticism of the One again in Hegel. If the One is infinite, then nothing can exist outside of it, because in order to exist the finite would have to exclude from itself the infinite, which would limit it in some way.

is by a certain neo-Platonic reading of Aristotelianism. This reading adapts the Aristotelian texts to a complex worldview not so much Christian but Islamic. Viewed in this way, Aquinas's image of himself as the defender of Aristotle against the misconstrued interpretations of Arab commentators is not completely without foundation. Christianity and Aristotelianism are conjoined in their defense of the finite and their refutation of the sublimation or annihilation of the finite by the infinite. Defending the legitimacy of the finite also establishes a certain affinity between Thomistic realism and a type of materialism that defends and protects the dignity of the finite by battling idealism. At the same time, realism is distinguished from this type of materialism by its balance in recognizing man's inherent tendency toward the infinite and the overcoming-of-self that materialism is essentially unable to embrace.

Idealism places reality at the level of abstract idea and depreciates matter and man himself as a material and finite being; it prefers the ideal category of "humanity." Materialism, on the other hand, maintains an opposition between the finite and the infinite but restores matter to its rightful dignity; nevertheless, materialism is powerless when confronted with the necessity of explaining the insufficiency of the finite and its tendency towards self-transcendence.

Thomistic realism reconciles the finite and the infinite by acknowledging that the finite is attracted by the infinite, but nonetheless retains its own proper consistency as it remains an irreducible "other." The deliberate *minutiae* of a philosophy that relies more on common sense than rhetoric yields a more adequate metaphysical justification for the notion of man as "tragic paradox" so magnificently and powerfully presented in the work of Pascal. The essential catholicity of Pascal is also very evident from this viewpoint.

On the other hand, this philosophy, so firmly anchored in common experience, also demonstrates more effectively the need for an integral understanding of man, for resolving the paradox man presents to himself, and for Christian revelation. The human drama emerging from the realist exercise of reason reaches its zenith in divine revelation, which reinforces natural reason and makes it more reliable. On the other hand, because this way of viewing man is so straightforward, demonstrable, and translucent in the light of reason, the allure of *divertissement* creeps in and inevitably sweeps man either toward idealistic presumption or a materialistic negation of his own grandeur. A historical-dialectical materialism seems to emerge from this apparent opposition between idealism and materialism which, in the face of realism, seems to hold great promise as an alternative way of reconciling two philosophical approaches that appear so incompatible.

Upon closer inspection, however, rather than a synthetic composition of idealism and materialism, historical-dialectical materialism seems to be a provisional and unstable compromise, a blending of materialistic and idealistic elements at a certain point in time and in a unique set of historical circumstances. When the spiritual fervor surrounding its inception began to fade, its hybrid quality also began to unravel into several different derivatives of idealism and materialism. Things are quite different in the case of realism. Here we have no trace of a compromise between idealism and materialism, but rather a very different philosophy that renders both one and the other intelligible.

Avicenna and Aquinas

As we turn to consider Avicenna's position in greater detail, we must first note that the categorical apparatus of the active and passive intellects is entirely restructured in his thought. If his fundamental thesis is the *unity* of the active intellect (in this he distances himself from Averroës), then the import of his thesis will only come to full light if we relate it to his rethinking of the possible intellect and its function. In fact, for Avicenna the possible intellect is not the *locus* where the forms known by the subject through experience are preserved. Rather, the species extracted from the phantasm by the agent intellect remains in the possible intellect only while the species is intuited in act. As soon as this intellective act passes, the species ceases to be joined to the possible intellect.

The material element of the species—that is, that which makes it correspond to the data of sense experience—is preserved in the faculty of memory, and it is through recourse to memory that the possible intellect returns to apprehend the species in act whenever necessary. Avicenna arrives at this conclusion by postulating that the forms, while remaining present in the faculty that corresponds to them, are apprehended by the same faculty when it is in act. The intelligence-in-act of the species—that is, the unity between the subjective capacity for knowledge and the external element that brings knowledge to completion—is therefore derived from the possible intellect's contact with the intelligible species; "[*I*]ntellectus *in actu est intellectum in actu*." This principle will be encountered again in Hegel's logic. The subjective and objective elements of knowledge coincide in the act of knowing.

Yet experience alone shows us that our intellect is not in a permanent active state with respect to every intelligible species with which it unites. Rather, in the case of most species, the intellect simply remains in a state of potency. It does not have the species present to itself, but neither is it in the same state with respect to another species it has not previously apprehended and therefore has yet to grasp for the first time.

According to Avicenna, the unique way in which the intellect exists in a state of potency cannot be explained in terms of the possible intellect alone. Insofar as it is spiritual and bereft of a bodily organ, the possible intellect is always and totally in act with respect to intelligible substance, and either in act or in potency with respect to the species. It cannot be conceived as a place in which known species are preserved after they cease to be known in act. Consequently, in addition to the *virtus apprehensiva,* we must posit the existence of a *thesaurus virtutis apprehensivae*: a place where the apprehended forms are preserved in a state of potency with respect to a new act of intellection by the possible intellect. According to Avicenna, the place where this occurs must have a material element, precisely because the forms within it are in a state of potency rather than act. The possible intellect is simply the memory. Just as in the imagination the apprehended forms are preserved through the senses, in the memory the apprehended forms are preserved independently from the senses through a process of intellectual abstraction.

Naturally, however, in a corporal faculty such as memory, the species can be preserved only as *intelligible in potency.* Therefore, there is no substantial difference—or, at most, there is only a difference of degree—between the way in which the form exists in the material object and the way in which it is preserved in the memory after the act of intellection. In both cases, it is in a state of potency within a material element. Consequently, every new knowing act requires a new intervention on the part of the agent intellect. Yet this new intervention on the part of the agent intellect is not to be conceived as abstraction from material preserved in the memory. If it were, there would be no way to distinguish between remembering a concept already apprehended and constructing it rationally through the mind's own functioning. In fact, the initial construction of the concept already utilizes materials preserved and arranged in memory. Avicenna, however, explains the difference by proposing that when the concept is recalled by memory, the intelligible form flows directly from the agent intellect into the possible intellect. It is easy to see that we are not merely dealing with a general theory about memory. Rather, by focusing on a specific question about the faculty of memory, Avicenna ends up overturning Aristotle's entire psychology.[106] If we admit that the intelligible species flows from the agent intellect to the possible intellect, then the notion of the agent intellect is completely transformed. It will no longer be thought of as the faculty that abstracts the intelligible species from the *phantasma,* but rather as the place where all the species are intelligible in act. Sense experience will no longer be the starting point for the knowing process but instead the occasion for the passing of the species from the agent intellect to the possible intellect.

In fact, when a concept is known for the first time, the phantasm has the sole function of rendering the active and passive faculties proportionate to one another. Through the knowing act, the agent intellect and the possible intellect acquire the perfect habit of conjoining themselves so that they can repeatedly arrive at new knowledge of a single identical object. The agent intellect, in which the species are already intelligible in act, takes the shape of a true separate substance that serves as the driving component in the cognitive process, and in which a knowable thing is already intelligibly present in act.

Even though this position is allegedly Aristotelian, and even though Avicenna, taking his cue from Aristotle, explicitly polemicizes the Platonic theory of the ideas, the substantial dependence of Avicenna's framework on Plato is undeniable.[107]

Plato held that the intelligible forms were separate substances constituting the source of all the soul's knowledge. Avicenna posits a single

106 Avicenna, *De Anima,* 5, c. 6.
107 Aquinas also makes reference to this in his refutation. See for example *Summa contra gentiles,* 2, c. 74.

separate substance as the origin of all knowledge. The difference he introduces, however, is *per se* of little consequence insofar as the structure of the
cognitive act remains essentially Platonic. The differences between them
are internal to this single general conception. According to Plato, knowledge is basically recollection. The ideas themselves always shed light on
what the human soul knows. The soul, however, oversaturated by the sensible and the particular, leaves behind every trace of the ideas. For Plato,
sensible experience was the occasion for this, since, by means of sense experience, the soul recalls that which it carried within itself from the beginning. Evidently, since the soul and separated substance are both of a
spiritual character, it is not possible to posit a sensible element, such as empirical knowledge, as the basis for the relationship between them. Indeed,
the original cause of the soul's forgetfulness—or the source of separated
substance's attenuated influence on the human soul—was the "turn" to the
sensible realm. Things are different for Avicenna. For him, when the possible intellect turns toward the phantasms contained in the imagination,
the agent intellect casts its light on the possible intellect, thus enabling it
to know the universal. The influence of the material part of the soul—i.e.,
the faculties of imagination, memory, and cognition—renders the possible
intellect capable of being affected by the agent intellect. Here we see a difference—and indeed a complete detachment—not only from Aristotle, but
also from traditional Platonism. In fact, it is through a negation of the sensible that the soul disposes itself to receive the influence of separated substance. If intelligible knowledge were *per se* the effect of separated substance,
then the actual mode of knowing the intelligible world would occur
through the negation of the sensible.

The only positive effect of sensible experience would be that of recalling
the need for this detachment. As a mode of knowledge, Aristotelian abstraction would be replaced by a simple negation of the finite.

Avicenna is still too Aristotelian to go so far as to reject completely the
theory of abstraction. Instead, he tries to posit a middle term between Plato
and Aristotle that will allow us to retain the value of the turn to the finite,
while at the same time maintaining total incommunicability between the
spiritual and sensible realms laid down by Plato. But in so doing, Avicenna
takes an important step toward the complete materialistic overturning of
Platonism. In fact, the soul's inferior faculties appear to be a decisive

element in closing the gap between the possible intellect and the agent intellect as the *locus* of the *intelligibilia* in act. This seems to be Ernst Bloch's point of attack in his interpretation of Avicenna's thought as presented in *Avicenna und die aristotelische Linke*. In any case, we must not forget that the Gnositc vision remains substantially unitary, regardless of whether it is presented in a materialistic or idealistic way. In the end, it is worth remembering that when we apply the term Platonism to Avicenna and Averroës, or when we try to refute either the Thomistic connection between Aristotelianism and Christianity or the Avicennian and Averroistic connection between Platonism and Gnosticism, the Platonism we have in mind is of a re-elaborated type that runs from Plotinus to Porphyry: it is a neo-Platonism with Gnostic tendencies. There is another, perhaps more legitimate reading of Plato offered by Augustine and Christian Platonism that remains a continuous point of reference for Aquinas's philosophy.[108]

Aquinas's critique of Avicenna begins by focusing on our understanding of the possible intellect, and similarly, of the human soul itself. In the first place, Aquinas observes that if, as everyone admits, the possible intellect is spiritual in itself, then it cannot receive forms in an unstable and provisionary way. In fact, if matter receives form, and the form remains in the matter for a certain period of time, it is all the more necessary to suppose a permanence of form (indeed, a stable and everlasting permanence) within a spiritual element once the matter has received it. The fundamental argument (to which we will return shortly) is strengthened by a careful consideration of the Aristotelian doctrine of matter. It is a basic Aristotelian tenet (in Book III of the *De anima*) that the point of departure for the knowing act is the phantasm, and that knowledge consists in abstracting forms from the matter to which the phantasms are conjoined. To deny this is to imagine that the species comes to the possible intellect from a separate substance; this idea completely overturns the Aristotelian position. The thesis concerning the primacy of the abstractive process is equally valid with regard to the first and original act of knowledge and to successive acts. This point is worth pondering for a moment. Avicenna's position, although not as clear as one would wish, can be interpreted in

---

108 On this topic, see Augustine, *De quantitate animae*, 23, 43; *De Genesi ad Litteram*, 1, 16, 31; *De Trinitate*, 9, 3, 3.

two different ways: in a neo-Platonic way or an Aristotelian way, as understood by Averroës. We can assume that the species comes into the possible intellect from the agent intellect through the work of the agent intellect which is activated only occasionally by the phantasms. Here we are closer to the Platonic theory of knowledge, according to which the agent intellect is the place where every species is contained from the beginning; that is to say that the agent intellect is in act from the outset with respect to all species. This makes the intellect quite similar to the divine *Logos*.

Alternatively, we can limit ourselves to saying that after the first act of knowledge the species, derived from reality by a process of abstraction, is preserved in the agent intellect. But if we consider this position carefully it appears less radical than the former. In fact, cognitive acts that abstract the species from matter will be relegated to the first stages of human existence. The "product" of these first cognitive acts, preserved in the agent intellect, is subsequently re-illuminated by the agent intellect in particular acts of knowing. We thus arrive at the same position as Averroës.

Finally, there is a moderate interpretation that stems from a modified version of Augustine's theory of *lumen* and that closely resembles the Thomistic interpretation. The agent intellect can be understood according to the metaphor of light. Light does not contain within itself the sensible forms of things but rather permits the eye to perceive sensible forms without identifying itself with them in any way.

Let us momentarily leave aside this solution to the problem and concentrate on the first two. The first is essentially a repetition of Plato, and the second is a recapitulation of Averroës. As mentioned previously, there is a connection between these two lines of thought and Hegelianism. But there is also an important difference. The role of time and its relationship to truth is absent from Avicenna. He conceives the Universal as logical-mathematical knowledge and not as historical knowledge. The result is that the original acquisition of the concept renders successive acts of knowledge by the meta-individual knowing substance superfluous. Things are different for Hegel. For him, each successive act of knowledge in history reaches an ulterior concrete determination of a universal that was originally abstract. This essential modification severely attenuates the philosophical value of Platonism. Originally, Platonism placed truth outside history and repudiated Christianity because it contains a certain "historicization" of truth (i.e.,

Jesus of Nazareth is the *Logos*). In Hegel, we encounter a complete overturning and historicization of truth. Hence Hegelianism can be considered
either as a sort of Platonism or the complete transformation of Platonism
by moving from eternal, transcendent ideas to a truth that attains its fulfillment in history.

Another angle of attack used by Aquinas to counter Avicenna regards
the faculty of memory. We have seen that Avicenna makes imagination the
thesaurus virtutis sensitivae and memory the *thesaurus virtutis intellectivae*.
Aquinas points out that not only does this contradict Aristotle's text, it is
self-contradictory in its very construction. The immaterial concept cannot
be preserved in a material faculty like the memory. Memory regards the
past, whereas concepts regard the universal. The universal cannot be contained only within a spiritual element. The Avicennian theory of memory
only appears to be in continuity with the Aristotelian theory of knowledge,
when in fact it is radically different from Aristotelianism.

So, what conclusion can we draw from this? Aquinas's conclusion is
not entirely clear. Let us look at the passage in question:

> *Intellectus enim possibilis est in actu perfecto secundum species
> intelligibiles cum considerat actu: cum vero non considerat actu, non
> est in actu perfecto secundum illas species, sed se habet medio modo
> inter potentiam et actum.*[109]

Of course, the difficulty is with the *medio modo inter potentiam et
actum*. Is it possible to think of an intermediate state between potency and
act? Perhaps consideration of the moral aspect of the question will help us
to understand what he means. The concept, which plays a central role in
the act of understanding, passes through a series of mediations before reaching the four fundamental ideas of the Good, the Beautiful, the True, and
the One. We have to ask ourselves how we come to know these four fundamental ideas. Knowledge of them spans the entire range of human cognition. In turn, each of them entails the others. Each contributes to the
perfection, or at least the presence, of all the transcendental ideas in the
human soul. Each concrete, individual experience therefore modifies the

---

109 *Summa contra gentiles*, 2, c. 74.

soul's spiritual substance, and every intellective act contains (potentially) in some way every act that precedes it. On the other hand, the *esse* implicitly contained in every particular concept of each individual knowing act does not detract from the fact that, if I want to *actually* think that concept, I must turn my attention to it explicitly.

With these observations in mind, we touch upon a fundamental problem that Aquinas never loses sight of—namely, the immortality of the human soul and its moral perfectibility. According to the Averroist position man has no spiritual soul. According to the Avicennian position, man has a spiritual soul (the possible intellect), but it is devoid of content and therefore bereft of personality. After death, the individual soul rejoins the universal soul by mixing with it. For Aquinas, however, every experience is preserved in the possible intellect. Consequently, every action performed throughout one's life actually modifies the spiritual substance of the human soul by making it better or worse, enhancing or diminishing its participation in the truth. Since they are preserved in man's spiritual element, these experiences do not disintegrate with the body at death. They continue to qualify the soul intrinsically. Even after the body dies, the soul remains the point of synthesis for the body's vital experience as its most perfect act. A sense of the good and evil performed in life remains and defines a person indefinitely. Future reward or punishment, as taught by Catholicism, is nothing other than the human soul's diaphanous self-knowledge of what it has wrought by its own activity. From this perspective, we can better understand what Aquinas means by *medio modo inter potentiam et actum*. To be in potency means that the single intelligible thing is absorbed, so to speak, into the stream of intellectual intuition. On the other hand, to be in act means to be caught up in the very act of thinking a thing's single, individual elements. Let us return for a moment to the comparison between Avicenna and Hegel we were making earlier.

Albeit in seminal form, there is a new element in Aquinas to which Hegel tied the entire destiny of his philosophy: time. That time should enter into the determination of truth is too heretical an idea within the entire classical tradition for us to find it enunciated in a provocative way by a philosopher as prudent and submissive to the authority of that same classical tradition as Aquinas. Nevertheless, it emerges with unambiguous necessity from his fundamental theses. The truth about man (his salvation) is wrought in time, and in time the soul receives its proper content. Neo-Platonism is correct to identify a *reditus* movement in God's nature, although this "return" is accomplished in the individual man; that is, the recapitulation of history occurs in the life of the individual who is ultimately reunited to God (or who eternally forfeits this *reditus* as the fulfillment of his destiny).

What Hegelian philosophy attributes to history, Thomistic philosophy attributes to the individual. The latter depends on the truth of Christian doctrine regarding the *immortality of the person* and on a definition of the person as formulated in terms of conscious action and freedom. Granted, the notion of the immortality of the soul can be found in other religions, both non-Christian and pre-Christian. Nevertheless, we need to stress emphatically the difference between the Christian position on immortality and the way it is seen from other religious viewpoints.

This difference is fleshed out through an understanding of man as *person*. Almost all primitive peoples believe in the soul's survival after death. But the spirit is usually considered a semi-corporeal substance, or a ghost, that poses a threat to the living. It lasts for a limited period of time before finally evaporating. Classical antiquity developed a more lofty idea of immortality: The human soul is already a spiritual element in itself and reunites with the earth's soul after death. While classical antiquity attributed a substantial soul to man, it did not believe that this substance was affected interiorly by the body's lived experience in history. Lived experience is basically irrelevant, at least insofar as the soul is estranged from the body. Reward and punishment are conceived as a definitive liberation from matter and a re-absorption into the impersonal spirit (e.g., Buddhist Nirvana) or as a re-immersion into the material and finite. This is similar to Avicenna's idea of non-personal immortality (i.e., a possible intellect devoid of content). In the end, Catholic teaching on the personal soul's immortality is utterly diverse from other religious conceptions (to a certain degree, so is Hebrew and Islamic teaching).[110] On the other hand, the personal soul's immortality (which always has a unique value attached to it, distinguishing it from other finite substances) begs for an investigation into the end and meaning of individual experience, since individual experience is itself

110 *Ibid.*, *Summa theologiae*, I, q. 75, a. 7; *Summa contra gentiles*, 2, c. 79.

contradictory and unresolved, as well as an investigation into the resurrection of the body. The soul, in fact, as the form of the body, cannot properly be subjected to God's judgment if the body is not restored to it, insofar as judgment is essentially a resolution of the contradiction characterizing the soul's earthly existence. The body, in turn, will be transfigured according to the judgment it will undergo on the basis of its earthly experience.

Consequently, in the first part of his critique against Avicenna, Aquinas reclaims the unique characteristics of the possible intellect *contra* Avicenna's attempt to eliminate them.

The second step of the critique is fairly simple. If man's cognitive function is so irrevocably apportioned between the agent intellect and the possible intellect—and if, moreover, the possible intellect is a faculty proper to the individual soul—then the same must be true of the agent intellect. It is in fact quite easy—indeed practically necessary—to think of the agent intellect as a separated substance once we admit that it is the *locus* where all the intelligible species are preserved in act. It is still possible to think of a "meta-individual" agent intellect that preserves within itself the species derived through abstraction from sensible reality. But it would be absurd to think of a pure faculty of abstraction subsistent in itself with no connection to the intellectual faculty that actualizes in itself—in act—the knowledge toward which the agent intellect's activity is directed.

Let us summarize the main points of Aristotelian metaphysics of knowledge as sketched above. Through the action of the agent intellect the phantasm becomes a *species intellegibilis in actu*. But a *species intellegibilis in actu* is not possible in itself apart from the act by which it is effectively apprehended, and this act pertains to the possible intellect. The activity of the agent intellect is limited to the abstraction of the species from the phantasm. There is no way the *species intellegibilis in actu* can be preserved outside the act of intellection and apart from the possible intellect.

If we follow a different line of reasoning, we would have to admit that the *species intellegibilis in actu* is not only abstracted by the agent intellect but also apprehended and preserved in the intellectual substance. This in fact is what Avicenna thought, but we have already seen the contradictions triggered by such a line of reasoning. There is no way to circumvent the fact that the agent intellect is not an autonomous power but a spiritual faculty of the soul.

After having confronted Avicenna's argumentation regarding the analysis of the principles of knowledge, Aquinas, in Chapter 76 of Book II of the *Summa Contra Gentiles,* cannot resist the urge to recall the fundamental axiom underlying his entire philosophical thought—namely, every being possess sufficient faculties for pursuing its proper end; that is, for performing the natural operations proper to it.[111]

Man's proper end is intellectual knowledge. If we were to claim that man is not proportioned to that end, or that he is able to pursue that end only with the help of a separate substance, we would deprive him of those faculties that specifically make him a man. This leads to some potentially disastrous results both from the point of view of anthropology and, for Christians, from the point of view of revelation and grace.

In fact, if the agent intellect were a separate substance, by nature it would be superior to man. The act of intelligence would essentially be supernatural and the order of nature would be completely confused with the order of revelation and grace. In order to perform a simple act of intelligence, man would necessarily require supernatural grace. We would be forced to conclude that the definition of man as intelligent and free is inappropriate or that God is forced by nature (a nature He himself created) to go beyond the order of nature in establishing a relationship with man in order to allow him to participate in the supernatural order.

In this case, to save the distinguishing human characteristics of intelligence and freedom, we are forced to deny God's freedom, and ultimately (if we continue in this vein) to deny human freedom, the very thing we set out to preserve!

On the other hand, from an Avicennian-Averroistic point of view, the unity of matter and form in the human being collapses, giving rise to the equivocal concept of "super-individual humanity." Aquinas concludes:

> *Si igitur intellectus agens est quaedam substantia extra hominem, tota operatio hominis dependet a principio extrinseco. Non igitur erit homo agens seipsum, sed actus ab alio. Et sic non erit dominus suarum operationum; nec merebitur laudem aut vituperium; et peribit tota*

111 See *Summa theologiae,* I, q. 79, a. 4.

scientia moralis et conversatio politica; quod est inconveniens. Non est igitur intellectus agens substantia separata ab homine.[112]

In the end, Aquinas corroborates his position with an observation about generative processes taken from the philosophy of Plato and Aristotle; it is an observation that reinforces the concordance of Aristotelian philosophy with the Christian anthropological vision. As we know, Plato acknowledges that the human soul is in a state of potency with respect to intelligible realities. He attributes a separate existence to the soul and makes its intellective act derive from contact with the world. If this position is correct, it would follow that the more intelligible a spiritual substance is in itself, the more directly and deeply this reality would have to be reflected in the human soul. If we pay careful attention to the way man turns to intelligible species, we see that he is most immediately impressed by those endowed with a more intense intelligible light. And since that which is supremely intelligible in itself is God, man should be completely imbued with that vision. This, however, does not accord with everyday experience. The order of intelligibility of the real *quoad nos* is in fact different from its order of intelligibility *in se*. It is precisely for this reason that Aristotle, in order to mirror in a modified way the effective movement of the soul toward knowledge, wants the universal to be the point of arrival for the movement that commences with sensible reality. It follows that the concept that first presents itself to the subject is not that which has maximum intelligibility in itself, but rather that which is closest to our sensible experience, and in that way it possesses greater intelligibility for us. On the other hand, because it is situated in matter, the form is intelligible for us only in potency.

From this it follows that *the agent intellect renders the form, immanent to material sensation, intelligible in act.* Here enters the theory of *lumen*, but the "light" in this case is different from the divine light under which the intelligibility of a thing is seen in itself. Here we are dealing with what Eliot calls "our little light": a light entirely internal to the realm of nature.[113]

While there was an unorthodox attempt to fuse the Augustinian position of *lumen* with the Avicennian theory of agent intellect, Aquinas

---

112 *Summa contra gentiles*, 2, c. 76.
113 *Choruses from "The Rock,"* 10.

separates the theory of the agent intellect from the *lumen* and reformulates it on the basis of Augustine's *lumen* model, while simultaneously maintaining a rigorous distinction. The key to his construction is the sharp distinction between intelligibility *in se* and intelligibility *quoad nos*. The agent intellect is indeed a light, but it is a *lumen proportionatum*.[114]

The Aristotelian-Thomistic way of expressing the agent intellect in terms of a *lumen proportionatum* does not necessarily exclude the possibility of a reformulated (though not equivocal) Augustinian theory of light in the face of Avicennism.[115] The problem can be reformulated along the lines of the following points: Does not knowledge by means of abstraction from sensible being perhaps negate the intelligibility of separated substances *in se* and of God himself? Does this, in turn, not create an insuperable abyss between man and God if the intelligibility of God cannot be infused into the human intellect?

Aquinas responds to these objections by making a comparison in the sensible realm. The human intellect in its composition of agent and possible intellect is comparable to the eye of a nocturnal animal as understood in mediaeval zoology. Mediaeval zoology maintained that the eye of a nocturnal animal was not only sensitive to light, but also irradiated a light of its own toward objects. These objects were perceived by the receptive faculty of the eye in the light emitted by the eye. Similarly, the agent intellect projects into the obscurity of matter its own ray, rendering the species, which is intelligible in matter (though only potentially), to be intelligible in act.

What happens to the eye of a nocturnal animal when exposed to sunlight? Because it is adapted only to its own weak light, it cannot perceive

114 See *De spiritualibus creaturis,* a. 10. Aquinas strives here to find a point of convergence with the Augustinian theory of *lumen*. He holds that the doctrine of the unicity of the agent intellect is a bit less absurd than the doctrine of the unicity of the possible intellect, that this unified agent intellect corresponding to the Augustinian *lumen* cannot be the same agent intellect of which Aristotle speaks, and that this agent intellect does not exclude the capacity of abstraction proper to the human soul as such. He confronts this problem more hastily both in the *Summa theologiae* and in the *Summa contra gentiles*. His position in the *De unitate intellectus contra Averroistas* is more intermediate.

115 See Thomas Aquinas, *Summa contra gentiles*, 3, c. 53; *Summa theologiae*, 1, q. 12, a. 5.

the object due to an overabundance of light. The same holds true for the human soul, and in particular for the possible intellect, with respect to the light emanating from intelligible substances and especially God. Since the possible intellect is equipped to see only in the light of the agent intellect, it can see the form immersed in matter and illuminated by the nocturnal light of the agent intellect, but it is not able to perceive intelligible substances in a light not its own. Such a light would be darkness for it. Here, once again, philosophy carries us to the immediate realm of theology, and in particular to the theological treatment of faith according to mystical theology.

In fact, we find the first traces of Saint John of the Cross's idea of the dark night of faith. Our intellect *"ad ea quae sunt manifestissima se habet sicut oculus noctuae ad solem."* One can perceive a trace of God in sensible reality, but it is impossible to have any intellectual intuition of Him. For such intuition to occur, there must be a *medium proportionatum,* and this intermediary between God and man is faith. By turning to the contents of faith and accepting them *in se,* although they are not fully and openly apparent to reason (but nevertheless not contradictory to reason, even though they transcend it), the human intellect assimilates itself to the divine intellect. In turning toward the divine light, the human intellect is blinded by it, unable to see anything (i.e., Saint John's dark night of the soul). But even here, through faith this "eye" is proportioned to its object, albeit obscurely. Through faith, the object is already present, and the subject is rendered capable of attaining union with God.

On the other hand, the theme of faith is strictly tied to the Incarnation. Faith, in fact, is faith in the incarnate Word, Jesus Christ. In the humanity of Christ, the Word is made perceptible to man, opening the possibility of an intimate relationship with him. Far from contradicting the theory of light, Aquinas's metaphysics of knowledge lays the groundwork so that his epistemological theory is not equivocated and interpreted in a way that would eliminate the necessity of faith. In this sense, despite all his Aristotelianism Aquinas is not completely unaffected by the pervasive and fundamental current of Christian Platonism that nourished Saint Augustine and the Church Fathers. The question of the relationship between faith and reason is also woven into the fabric of these other questions. In fact, it is practically identical to the question of the relationship between the agent intellect and the *lumen* since it involves two different epistemological principles, each of which has its own distinctive methodological autonomy, but both of which refer to an identical object. Just as the material object perceived at night by means of a ray of light emanating from a nocturnal animal's eye is the same object perceived under the sun's light during the day, so the concepts man perceives by the light of the active intellect are the same as perceived by the light of faith. The methodological autonomy of these two principles does not inevitably imply an absolute separation between faith and reason such that faith has nothing to say about the natural realities man has access to by exercising his own powers. The closer these natural realities are to the ethical order of man's existence and salvation (in view of which revelation is given to him), the more the same object can and must be considered both in the light of natural reason and the light of faith. But there is also a certain distinction between these two areas. Revelation, given to man for the sake of his salvation, does not extend to the whole gamut of reality and is therefore only indirectly related to things other than the human person. On the other hand, human reason does not extend to forms beyond sensible objects, and therefore does not directly touch upon either spiritual substances or God. Furthermore, human reason has a precarious knowledge of material reality, just as nocturnal animals know things only in the dark and not in the light.

On the other hand, knowledge by the light of faith is still obscure. It comes about through an adaptation of the human intellect to the divine light, but this process is never finished. In this life, the *lumen Christi* is different from the *lumen gloriae*, the latter being knowledge of God himself and all earthly things and their perfect truth in his light. From these considerations we can draw three conclusions:

1) Faith and reason never truly contradict one other.
2) The spheres of faith and reason overlap, though only partially. This overlapping primarily regards human realities and the human soul's tendency toward truth and goodness.
3) Apparent and provisional conflicts between reason and faith are always possible either because of undue crossing-over from one epistemological domain to the other, or because of the obscurity of reason and faith in this life.

These clarifications help to counter the temptation to allow the intellect's individual knowing acts to be absorbed into a type of knowledge of the whole proper to faith. They also counter the presumption that reason is the sole principle of knowledge and the labeling of the knowledge proper to faith as "unknowable." Such clarifications also help to keep at bay the idea of a double truth—namely, an idea that essentially implies a radical difference between the forms of things as they exist in matter and are known through abstraction, and the forms of things as contained in the mind of God.[116] Finally, these clarifications oppose the doctrine of a complete separation between the realms of faith and reason due to their respective objects. The first and last of these positions are particularly relevant today. The first is presented in two different versions. The first coincides with what is usually referred to as integralism. Faith is extolled as the only adequate principle for knowing the *societas,* and the weak intellective light proportioned to our natural knowledge is subsumed into the infinite light of God. This position was more fully developed by the great reactionary philosophies of history found in Joseph de Maistre and Louis Gabriel Ambroise de Bonald.

The other position—i.e., the third of the above three—lies outside Catholicism and is represented principally in the philosophy of Hegel and similar schools of thought. According to this way of thinking, the Spirit—that is, God's intelligible light that alone illuminates history—is conceived as naturally proportioned to the human intellect, which receives the Spirit into itself, thereby obtaining complete knowledge of the world and itself.

A common characteristic of both these versions is the elimination of any difference between nature and grace. According to the integralist position, nature is completely incapable of truth since the capacity to know the truth is attributed entirely to grace. According to the Hegelian position, grace is absorbed into nature. Both positions attribute a totalitarian knowledge either to Humanity or to the Church (depending on which version you choose), implying that the created realm has a capacity for both self-knowledge and knowledge of God's creative action, and consequently that the created realm has the ability to reach perfect knowledge of absolute truth. The Hegelian principle of a perfect identity between subject and object is disclosed through absolute knowledge.

116 *Summa contra gentiles*, 1, c. 4; *Summa theologiae*, I, a. 1.

Here we can retrace a certain parallel between Aquinas's position and the conclusions reached by the so-called Frankfurt School (at least as represented by Max Horkheimer) in the latter's critique of Hegelianism and Hegelian Marxism.[117] In Aquinas we have a systematic reconstruction of the unique type of knowledge proper to man. Human knowledge is neither reduced to a pure reconstruction of mechanistic connections, nor is it minimized to the pure instrumentality proper to the passive intellect. Moreover, Aquinas's system refuses to qualify the human intellect through knowledge of a kind of "universal intrinsic finalism" in the cosmos. Man individuates structures in nature, including structures with a particular *telos* or goal, but these are regional or particular finalisms and not the cosmic finalism of nature as a whole. The agent intellect gives the knowing subject an ability to grasp the structure and form of particular realms of experience, but between these and the totality of intelligible experience lies a gap the human intellect is powerless to bridge. By reflecting on the internal and external properties of experience, the subject can formulate general rational hypotheses about the fundamental characteristics inherent in nature that articulate the being-ness of the world, but nothing more. We thus come back to a fundamental thesis: By the power of his natural reason man can know that God exists, but he is unable to know what God is. That is, he is unable to know the essence and structure of the "being-ness" of God.

When we reconsider some of the fundamental theses of Max Horkheimer, it is striking how similar he is to Hegel on several points. He refuses, on the one hand, to apply the principle of identity between subject and object to the movement of human knowledge, and, on the other hand, he foregoes adopting a merely mechanistic vision of existence; and finally, he also refuses to accept the Kantian solution of separation that attributes knowledge of the infinite to a particular and autonomous intellectual faculty rather than viewing it as a synthesis emerging from the entire cognitive process.

There are positive elements mixed in with these more readily recognizable negative elements. For example, there is the attribution to the human intellect of the capacity to know the structures and forms hidden within

---

117 See Rocco Buttiglione, *Dialettica e Nostalgia* (Milano: Jaca Book, 1978), which examines Max Horkheimer's thought and its religious significance.

material realities; an emphasis on the necessity of the infinite, or rather the negative relation between the activity of thinking and infinity; a refusal to admit that through man's initiative the infinite can be transformed from something negative into something positive. In this way, an area of distinctively human knowledge is established (i.e., a sort of natural, "partial finalism") that is open to God's transcendence.

In the realm of nature, the human soul is properly directed toward the knowledge of sensible objects, their forms, and the arrangement of their forms within the intelligible order. However, this intelligible order always presents itself to human reason in a defective and partial way, since by knowing things in the world man is simultaneously directed to knowledge of himself—a radical understanding of himself, his origin, the meaning of his existence and his destiny. We can think of this tendency of the human soul as a kind of nostalgia generating a dialectical movement, a disquietude of thought that cannot rest in any one particular finite object.

At the same time, as our preceding analysis has shown, there is always a twofold determination to the knowing act. On the one hand, it is directed toward things, making their forms exist in the human soul. On the other hand, it is directed toward the soul itself, modifying its spiritual substance by driving its process of self-knowledge forward. This process culminates in the understanding a soul possesses of its own spiritual nature, and consequently its capacity to relate to the infinite—a process mediated by the transcendental ideas (the true, the good, the beautiful, and the one), each of which helps to bridge the gap between the finite and the infinite, and each of which possesses an infinite value participated in some limited way by created things. The knowing process thus culminates in the understanding that each person's existence is rooted in the creating Mystery that places the true, the good, the beautiful, and the one into the world. This is the key supporting idea that underlies the doctrine of our negative knowledge of God and forces us to pause and reflect.[118] Conversely, it is impossible to know God, even if only negatively, without the simultaneous desire to relate to him in the most intense way possible.

---

118 This knowledge is negative, but it is not absolute non-knowledge. For this reason Aquinas should not be considered antithetical or incompatible with Anslem and Scotus on the issue of pure perfections.

We cannot pass this desire off as a kind of audacious presumption (it would be more accurate to say that God surpasses the light of the agent intellect and blinds the receptive capacity of the possible intellect, than it would be to say that He is the proper object of the soul's knowledge). We must rather accept it as a vital reality. This is the paradox of Catholic faith: While it acknowledges the truth of man's intentional stretching toward the infinite, at the same time it denies that faith can be given within this context alone. Rather, faith is the result of God's free initiative. Aquinas expresses this in his teaching that man, as he reaches the peak of his own spiritual activity, stimulates and nourishes the knowledge—however imperfect—that he can have of God rather than the perfect knowledge he can have of the objects naturally available to his cognitive abilities. This leads to yet another element within the paradox: Man knows material things in a spiritual way. Finally, it is necessary to note the affinity of Aquinas's theory to one particular aspect of Kantian philosophy—namely, the idea that within the human person there is a natural longing for the Infinite that can never be given to him as an object *per se*. Aside from the absence of a theology of grace, Kant differs from Aquinas in that for him this empty capacity for knowledge, besides being unable to penetrate the essence of its object, cannot even give a reason for the object's real existence.

Finally, in order to explain the proximity between Aquinas and the Frankfurt School, we must recall the Jewish background of the latter's philosophy. The Frankfurt philosophy is one which, because of the ambiguous way it approaches the problem of God (an inevitable ambiguity because of its refusal to root itself in monotheism), is not so much a *rapprochement* to Aquinas as a movement toward Maimonides, the great Jewish doctor of the Middle Ages who had many points in common with Aquinas.

Consequences of the Thomistic position

In order to clarify further the question of the intellect's unity, we must first review a series of decisive theses Aquinas held regarding the human soul, theses which essentially amount to his theory of the human person.

The first of these concerns the soul's immortality. The soul finds its completion or perfection in an act that is spiritual by its very nature. As we have already seen, the soul maintains its individuality even when separated from the body. The human soul is in fact the human body's specific form—specified not by the matter of the body but by its internal suitability to be united with a particular body; in other words, as the specific form of the body's "history." When the activity of the body terminates and ceases to possess the ability to acquire intelligible content from sense experience, the soul comes to full self-knowledge of the way it is transformed through its own activity.[119]

In fact, from the Thomistic viewpoint we have outlined thus far, the soul's action has a twofold effect: It modifies man's external reality while simultaneously modifying the soul's substance. Through his own action man defines his spiritual physiognomy. He initiates an activity proper to him through a sensible intuition of the body, but his experience progressively develops through knowledge of spiritual values and their actualization in his own spiritual substance. The soul, in the way it subsists *post mortem,* is precisely a notional knowledge of the person's history—the actualization, or lack thereof, of the human actions he has performed. The soul endures as a recapitulation of the person's entire history, replete with meaning and seared with a sense of one's entire life.

Here, however, we encounter an odd paradox in Aquinas. The word "history" never appears. I have said that the soul is qualified by the history it has lived out in its substantial unity with the body, but this way of formulating the question, although faithful to Aquinas's intention, is nevertheless my own and not that of Aquinas. He prefers to speak of a *commensuratio* of the soul to the body, the latter of which acts as the soul's principle of individuation. We also find this line of reasoning with particular lucidity, among other places, in Chapter 81 of Book II of the *Summa Contra Gentiles.* The problem Aquinas confronts is once again the possibility of preserving the individuation of the soul after its separation from the body. Once more, this harkens back to a fundamental problem central to

119 See *Summa theologiae,* I, q. 75, ad 3; 1, q. 89; I-II, q. 5, a. 1, ad 2; I-II, q. 67, a. 2c, ad 1 and ad 3; III, q. 2, a. 2. Aquinas strongly emphasizes the divine intervention that allows for the apprehension of intelligible species and other separated substances. While granting the presence of intellected species in this life, he attributes less importance to this element than we have insisted on here. In this way, I have tried to initiate a certain development of Aquinas's position in a way faithful to his thinking.

the Averroist controversy. If there were in fact no principle of identity for the human soul when it is separated from the body, then we would have to accept the Averroistic thesis of the spiritual soul's meta-individuality. Aquinas resolves the problem by recalling the entire course of reasoning we have already examined:

> *Non enim quaelibet formarum diversitas facit diversitatem secundum speciem, sed solum illa quae est secundum principia formalia, vel secundum diversam rationem formae: constat enim quod alia est essentia formae huius ignis et illius, nec tamen est alius ignis neque alia forma secundum speciem. Multitudo igitur animarum a corporibus separatarum consequitur quidem diversitatem formarum secundum substantiam, quia alia est substantia huius animae et illius: non tamen ista diversitas procedit ex diversitate principiorum essentialium ipsius animae, nec est secundum diversam rationem animae; sed est secundum diversam commensurationem animarum ad corpora; haec enim anima est commensurata huic corpori et non illi, illa autem alii, et sic de omnibus. Huiusmodi autem commensurationes remanent in animabus etiam pereuntibus corporibus: sicut et ipsae earum substantiae manent, quasi a corporibus secundum esse non dependentes. Sunt enim animae secundum substantias suas formae corporum: alias accidentaliter corpori unirentur, et sic ex anima et corpore non fieret unum per se, sed unum per accidens. Inquantum autem formae sunt, oportet eas esse corporibus commensuratas. Unde patet quod ipsae diversae commensurationes manent in animabus separatis: et per consequens pluralitas.*[120]

120 *Summa contra gentiles,* 2, c. 80. "For the diversity of species is not caused by an arbitrary diversity of forms, but precisely by a diversity according to formal principles or a difference in the *ratio* of the form: For clearly there is a difference between the essence of the form of this fire and of that fire, even though there is neither another fire nor another form of the fire according to species. Therefore, a plurality of souls separated from bodies follows upon a diversity of forms according to substance, for the substance of this soul is different from that one. Nevertheless, this diversity does not proceed from a diversity of the soul's essential principles, nor is it based on a different *ratio* of souls; rather, it is based on a different commensuration of souls to the body. For this soul is

I beg the reader's pardon for the lengthy Latin citation, but I think the passage is indispensable for a complete understanding of both the strength and weakness of Aquinas's proof for the immortality of the soul. Retracing the line of argument, we can say that the plurality of forms does not necessarily entail a plurality of species. The forms of sensible objects are differentiated by individuation according to the particular objects to which they refer, though without in any way compromising the unity of the species. The form is specified by the substrate of which it is the form—that is, by the *hypokeimenon,* to use Aristotle's term. It is precisely this that differentiates an object's substantial form from an attribute that may or may not be present, or an attribute that refers to one determined object and not another. The substantial form of the object, individuated by the object itself, is something distinct from the species understood as a logical category—that is, it is a universal concept present in the mind of the human knower.

With respect to the divine intellect, the species is the ultimate foundation for the existence of a substantial form; the substantial form, in turn, is the basis for the existence of the species as it exists in the human soul. This same line of reasoning can be used for the human soul, which itself is the body's substantial form. Granted, in this case we are dealing with a spiritual substance, although it is a spiritual substance united to a physical body as its substantial form. If the soul, therefore, insofar as it is a spiritual substance, does not dissipate with the death of the body, then, insofar as it is a substantial form, it is appropriated to "this" particular body—that is, to "this" particular man—even after the particular human body ceases to exist. This gives rise to the theory of the soul's *commensuratio* with the body: The soul endures even after the body's disintegration.

> commensurate to this body and not to that one, and that soul to this one and not that one, and so on. Moreover, commensurations of this type remain in souls even as they depart from bodies: Their substances likewise remain, as if not depending on bodies. For souls are the forms of bodies according to their (i.e., the souls') substances: Otherwise, they would be united to bodies accidentally, and in this way the body and soul would not make up a single entity *per se,* but *per accidens.* Insofar as they are forms, however, it is necessary that they be commensurate to bodies. From this it is clear that the same diversity of commensurations is also found in separated souls, for which reason there is a plurality of them."

The error of those who deny the soul's immortality, and in particular of those who choose not to admit the perdurability of the soul's individuality after death, always boils down to an error committed by Averroës: That is, it places a wall of separation between the reason for which the human soul is a spiritual substance and the reason for which it is the substantial soul of the body. Having constructed, more or less unknowingly, this wall of separation, and taking it as a presupposition, those who hold this position also believe that the substantial form of the body falls into nothingness after the death of the body.

However, the spiritual substance does indeed remain, although it is a spiritual substance deprived of all its individual determinations. Hence it can only be individuated through the species. But seeing as it is not possible to attribute a different species to every individual human soul, these naysayers are forced to admit the unicity of a spiritual principle. In order to better grasp the main point of Aquinas's defense of the soul's individuality, it would be worth recalling the Boethian definition of the person: *rationalis naturae individua substantia.* This classic definition involves a *hypokeimenon,* a real substrate that enjoys an autonomous existence with a rational nature. Confronted with the tendency to turn the soul into a fragment of a larger, single and impersonal spirit, Aquinas redeems the soul's substantiality and real subjectivity.

However, he never fully explains precisely in what this subjectivity consists. I have permitted myself to specify this substantiality as "history," and more precisely as the history of the person. The substantial form of the body is in fact a dynamic principle that pushes the body toward the fullest realization of its inherent potentialities. In conformity with the perfectionist principle in Thomistic ethics, we must then say that the soul is the dynamic principle that propels man toward the full actualization of his capacity for intelligence and freedom. The movement that expresses this yearning is the succession of events and moral choices that make up his life. In short, it is the history of the individual. In his history, man brings about the perfection of his own soul which is precisely the way he actualizes his unique dignity.

In order to do this, man is called to discern the various goods he encounters and which vie for his attention. The fulfillment of the human person's value consists in the actualization of the individual values he or she encounters in lived experience. For a greater appreciation of the depth of

the Thomistic formulation, we need only to glance at the organizing structure of the *Summa Contra Gentiles.* In this work, a general theory of the soul
is developed in Book Two immediately after the treatment of God's creation.
Then, in Book Three, he proceeds to demonstrate that every acting being
acts in view of an end, and that the end in view of which man acts is beati-
tude; that is, the knowledge of God. The ensuing demonstration relative to
the human soul, its spiritual character, and its autonomy with respect to the
body does not contradict its substantial unity with the body, and in fact is
a preliminary and absolutely indispensable condition for an adequate consideration of man's natural inclination toward the Good, his natural desire
to see God. According to Aquinas, this is the fulcrum upon which morality
turns. It is impossible to construct a moral theory if we do not begin with
the fact that man's activity leads him to either improve or ruin his soul, and
that he has a natural inclination toward the Good and toward God.

Conceiving morality in this way, however, means to conceive it histor-
ically. Man is essentially made up of his history—from the concrete good
and evil actions he performs in this life. But, as already noted, the word
"history" never appears in Aquinas's *opus.* We come to a terminal point in
his discussion of the soul's commensurability with the body, and we are
given no further development of what the principle means dynamically in
terms of history, and no attention is given to the historical aspect of the individual human person. Nor is it simply a matter of terminology, for
Aquinas *does* use the word "history." He simply does not offer an adequate
development of the concept.

We therefore find ourselves facing a paradox. Aquinas rigorously develops an objective foundation of personalism—that is, of the concept "person." In confronting the dangerous tendency toward Gnosticism he defines,
in an incomparable way, the philosophical basis for Christian anthropology.
And yet, throughout his works, we are hard pressed to see the concrete acting of the person, his moving about in the world. The ontological treatment
of the problem remains somewhat detached from affective experience and
the value of moral experience as Aquinas presents them. It is thus compart-
mentalized from the emotional experience of moral value each of us knows
directly. It is as if we were watching a replay in slow motion. Concrete man
appears rigid in a series of loosely connected frames that fail to flow with
the fluidity of real life. Time is missing, and with it, history.

Yet Aquinas alludes to this shortcoming. The way in which he conceives of and frames ethical questions necessarily involves an element of time: That is, it involves the use of an objective ethic, developed by departing from a metaphysical analysis of the human soul that serves as the basis for a full-fledged epistemological and anthropological theory. As we shall later see, it is at this point that the unique and essential complementarity of phenomenology and existential analysis (both of which are in a privileged position to enhance the metaphysics of personhood) emerges.[121] Pascal's existential analysis—to cite an example to which we have had frequently recourse—puts Aquinas's metaphysical categories in motion, connecting them with the affectivity of the human condition. Before elaborating the unique points of Thomistic personalism, we should highlight another salient result of the Averrroistic controversy—namely, the recovery of a "personality" for God alongside the personal character of his relationship to man. There is, in fact, a necessary and inextricable nexus connecting man's existence as a person to God's existence as a person. To the extent that man is a person and therefore capable of entering into personal relationships with other persons, he is also in a position to recognize God as a person. If, on the other hand, we move from the level of epistemology to ontology, we must admit that God, insofar as he is a person, creates man as a personal being so that man can enter into friendship with Him precisely as a relationship between persons. By way of negation, we can further substantiate this claim by noting that philosophical positions that deny the personality of God also deny the personality of man. We encounter this negation in antiquity beginning with a Manichean brand of Gnosticism. We have already mentioned the Manichean dualism of light and darkness and how, insofar as the soul is opposed to matter, the former is a flicker of divine light immersed in the obscurity of the latter, eagerly waiting to be set free. From the viewpoint of Manichean Gnosticism, the affairs of the world are characterized by a succession of infinite cycles, each of which is marked by an initial infusion of divine light generously mixed with matter, permeating and elevating it until a maximum level of co-penetration of light and darkness is finally reached, so that all the matter in the world is

121 Cf. Karol Wojtyła, *"Personalizm Tomistyczny,"* in *Znak*, 3 (1961), pp. 664–675.

eventually and completely spiritualized. This magic equilibrium, however, is sooner or later interrupted. Radically detached from its origin, the light loses itself in matter and becomes absorbed by it.

In this way, rather than rendering matter transparent, light is obscured by matter. The rays farthest from the origin grow weaker and dimmer to the point that they lose all knowledge of their particular nature. This forgetfulness signifies a new historical epoch in which darkness emerges triumphant. But since it is the presence of light that gives form to the material realm, the greater the dispersion of light in matter, the weaker the form. This dissipation of light plunges the world into chaos, and the elements that were once imprisoned in the substantial forms of things return in freedom, reuniting with one another in kind of primordial affinity. This process also frees the light that had been mixed with the world's darkness, allowing it to return to its original unity. Then the cycle can start over again. In this ultimate phase, the guiding spirit plays a fundamental role, sending the light from the center outwards towards the darkness to collect the scattered fragments of light that, saved from cosmic catastrophe, seek their way home. We have already seen how the Averroistic-Avicennian theory of the separated intellect is itself a particular variation of this Gnostic theme. In both cases, the metaphor of light tacitly devalues the role of personal knowledge.

Granted, we encounter the same metaphor in Christian authors. There, however, the light is always emitted from a source and referred back to that source. In the same way, knowledge has a precise subject endowed with its own autonomous personality. According to the Manichean theory, knowledge and light are hypostatized with respect to their subject; we end up with an impersonal light and an impersonal knowledge or understanding. Against his hypostatization, and in defense of the Christian concept of the person, Aquinas re-proposes the fundamental Aristotelian principle that there are no actions or qualities without a real substrate to support them: the Stagyrite's *hypokeimenon*.

The person is the actual substratum of knowledge; so much so that there is no knowledge if there is no person. This is just as true for man as it is for God, although in a wholly different way. The faculty responsible for forming the concept—the spiritual activity of the soul—presupposes the soul's substantial existence, an existence guaranteed by the soul as the form of a body. Consequently, there is no such thing as human knowledge that does not at the same time belong to a determinate man tied to a determinate body. Similarly, God's "knowledge" of ideas is conceivable only as an expression of the personhood of God who, in turn, is their actual substrate.

From this derives the idea of "God-as-mystery-for-man," the "mystery" here meaning personal life. The Gnostic position also speaks of God-as-mystery: God's knowledge is infinitely vaster than man's to the extent that, from the human point of view, God's knowledge necessarily remains mysterious. But this has nothing to do with a merely quantitative difference. Moreover, it is not a difference that depends solely on the fact that God's knowledge is of an archetypical character while man's is only "ectypical." Rather, we are face-to-face with a mystery that has a fundamental qualitative aspect rooted in the qualitative similarity between man and God. It is in fact the mystery of personal freedom. It is a mystery the depths of which we can never fathom. But it is nevertheless a mystery that man, due of his personal character, can comprehend in some small way by analogy. It is against this background that Aquinas situates his doctrine of analogy as a principle that allows for intercommunicability between God and men. It is also from the same depths that the affirmation "God is love" takes shape in Christianity, since love is the only modality through which the depth of personal experience can be communicated.

By opposing the Gnostic-Manichean idea, Aquinas not only affirms the difference between God and man (preserving in this way God's transcendence with respect to man), he also lays the groundwork for the affirmation of a similarity between man and God. This similarity, this profound dialogue launched by neo-Platonism, rests on the fundamental presupposition of the autonomous ontological solidity of the human person in the face of God, and therefore on the difference between God and man. Precisely insofar as they are different—that is, insofar as they are distinct *persons*—God and man encounter each another in a reciprocal act of free, self-giving love.

Thomistic scholars have not always reached the core of his intent and consequently have at times failed to recognize the indissoluble connection between these two constitutive elements of his thought. As a result, the notion of a distinction between God and man has been formulated and proposed almost to the point of negating man's constitutive impulse to transcend the order of simple material reality. That is to say, if we separate the natural from the supernatural, we run the risk of reviving a type of radical division between man's soul and his materiality—a division Aquinas himself had gone to great lengths to refute during the Averroist controversy. Of course, we do not want to negate the fundamental distinction between the natural and supernatural orders, nor do we find such a negation in Aquinas; but it must be emphasized that it is not possible to force the distinction between the natural and the supernatural to align neatly with the distinction between material reality and spiritual reality. Man is in fact a being who participates in a spiritual nature to the point that any attempt to limit his dynamism to the material realm will inevitably fail to yield a satisfactory and complete notion of his uniqueness. Aquinas's doctrine of the *desiderium naturale videndi Deum* stands precisely as a defense of the human person's spiritual character.

Space does not permit us to plumb the depths of the problem here.[122] Nevertheless, to take up this theme means to accept a Platonic religious affirmation that fascinated Augustine—namely, man is not made merely for the finite and will never discover his ultimate satisfaction in the finite. *Inquietum est cor nostrum donec in te requiescat Domine.* The battle against Avicennism and Averroism—far from contradicting this Augustinian tension and from limiting the human soul to finitude by allowing only the intervention of grace (understood in a magical way) to elevate man above the finite—places the paradox of man on more solid footing between the finite and the infinite. It binds him to a physical body but still grants him the ability to perform spiritual acts. Man, in fact, reaches his ultimate end only through a spiritual act that is structurally oriented toward a personal dialogue with God.

---

122 Despite the textual evidence, this problem in Aquinas's thought has been long neglected. See Henri de Lubac, *Augustinianism and Modern Theology* (New York: Herder and Herder, 2000). In particular, see the chapter entitled "Pure Nature and Natural Desire." See also M. Matthys, "*Quid ratio naturalis doceat de possibilitate visionis beatae secundum S. Thomas in Summa contra Gentiles,*" *Divus Thomas,* 3 (1936), pp. 201–228; Matthijs Mannes, *Quomodo anima humana sit "naturaliter capax gratiae" secundum doctrinam S. Thomae,*" *Angelicum,* 14 (1937), pp. 175–193; Jorge La Porta, *Le destinée de la nature humaine selon S. Thomas d'Aquin* (Paris: Vrin, 1965).

Concluding considerations

According to the Boethian definition, embraced by Aquinas, a person is a *rationalis naturae individua substantia,* an individual substance or substrate *(hypokeimenon)* of a rational nature. The individuality of the substrate is guaranteed by its connection to a physical body to which the human soul is "commensurate." This gives us a clear context for addressing the problem of the soul's relationship to the body and of the person's relationship to material reality. The criterion for the individualization of the person in comparison with other spiritual realities is also situated within this context. But if we define the person on the basis of what makes him similar to other natural beings and then top him off with an immaterial, substantial soul, we will never reach a satisfactory conclusion. Such a definition does not allow us to view the person as acting concretely in the realm of lived experience. It lacks that certain element that makes Augustine's approach to personhood so appealing. The person acts uniquely in the realm of created beings.

This entails a specific difference that most radically constitutes the human person and delineates clearly the principle of his individuation. At the same time, the principle of individuation as described by Aquinas is left wanting since it fails to elaborate on the crucial aspect of interpersonal relationship. It does not fully enter the world in which our attention is focused primarily on persons and the reciprocal relationships among them. Interpersonal relationship requires each person to overcome, so to speak, his or her limits of individuation, making room for an existence in the other and an allowance for the other to exist in itself. Only by raising the interpersonal aspects of the problem to an ontological level—indeed, only by affirming and esteeming the person's self-transcendence as evidenced through ontological analysis—will the personal relationships that constitute man and give him life allow us to adopt a more realistic, dynamic, and convincing vision of the person's real existence. The analysis we have carried out here helps to keep the ambiguities and misunderstanding about the notion of personal experience at bay, although it fails to put interpersonal experience in sharp focus.

For this reason, personalist philosophy has been somewhat critical of the excessive abstractness it perceives in Thomistic philosophy. This criticism certainly deserves a sympathetic ear, especially when directed toward the aspects of Aquinas's thought considered above. However, might this criticism be motivated, at least in part, by a certain mistake? Given Aquinas's unique systematic approach, might it still be possible to carry out a Thomistic analysis of the subjective aspect of personal experience? It seems to me that this subjective aspect is not completely absent from Aquinas's thought. It seems to lay hidden in his philosophy of spiritual substances: his so-called "angelology."

Substantial intellects, by their very nature, are intelligent. The question of intelligibility is usually approached through a comparison of the intellectual substance and its concepts. This, at least in part, was Aristotle's method. Through its concepts, an intellectual substance can work its way up the conceptual ladder to attain the transcendental ideas of the true, the beautiful, the good, and the one as ubiquitously present in the objective forms of the world and in the human intellect, as well as their perfect way of existing in the divine intellect. Plato gave concepts an ontological consistency when he proposed the ideas. Later, he tried to reduce the ideas to a single entity by developing an analogy between idea and number. Every idea is a participation or stage—a "number"—in the soul's ascent to the fundamental ideas mentioned above. Aristotle, in his doctrine of separated substances, begins with this Platonic idea and, using his own distinctive method, gives a real substrate and *individua substantia* to Plato's ideas. Later still, in Aquinas's approach to the problem, we find that he confers personal consistency to separated substances: A separated substance is a person in whom the grades of the good, the beautiful, the true, and the one inhere, giving meaning to the universe. This is also how the schoolmen of the Middle Ages read the scriptural passage, "The angels sing the glory of God." At a level infinitely higher than intelligibility, the perfection of separated substances expresses the glory of God through whom all things exist.

Aristotle did not fully develop the implications that stem from attributing Plato's ideas to a personal substance. For example, he does not expound the moral responsibility associated with personal being. This theme is rather taken up by Christian thinkers who, referring to Scripture, propose a division of separated substances into angelic and diabolic substances. At its core, the personal being's way of existing consists in making free decisions. This includes the decision to acknowledge one's own place within the universal order and therefore one's own determined participation in the existence of the real world. It means either accepting one's existence as a reflection of the universe's gradation of perfections, or closing oneself off from the world and living as a self-sufficient entity in pursuit of an autonomous end apart from, or in opposition to, other created things. The person has the ability to conceive of himself as a being open to communion with other personal beings. This, in turn, presupposes a preliminary, sincere recognition of a personal being underlying the order of the created universe—namely, God. Conversely, a person may choose to close himself off by refusing to acknowledge his own immanence and "presence" in other personal beings as well as their presence and immanence in his own interiority.

A choice against communion does not eliminate the fact that separated substances are an expression of a level of perfection in the universe. Nevertheless, a choice against communion leads to a loss of a "level" within the perfection of the universe—one of the *loci* where the creature's freedom fails to correspond to God's loving plan. The more perfect a being, the more easily it can yield to the temptation of living according to an ontological self-sufficiency that the Christian tradition calls pride or falsehood—"pride" because it pretends to have no need of submitting to God and acknowledging his presence as a horizon of existence where everything has its proper consistency and life, "falsehood" because it denies the fundamental truth that God exists and is the good of every creature.

The possibility of denial opened up by freedom breaks apart the monolithic—and in a certain sense constrictive—order of the Platonic-Aristotelian universe, insofar as it discloses, alongside the natural and spiritual order, a distinct and more essential order of grace. Lucifer, first among the angelic substances, is also the author of sin. In the order of moral perfection, the one who originally occupied first place then plummeted to the lowest through sin and becomes the Tempter and Prince of Lies, while the "dullest," the one most deficient in natural ability—namely, man—can now raise himself above Lucifer by making good moral choices.

The world in which we live is composed of many objects. The word "object" here means more or less the same as "entity." This is not the proper meaning of the word, since an "object," strictly speaking, is something related to a "subject." A "subject" is also an "entity"—an entity that exists and acts in a certain way. It is then possible to say that the world in which we live is composed of many subjects. It would indeed be proper to speak of "subjects" before "objects." If I have reversed the order in this book, my intention is to emphasize the objectivism or realism of the approach herein. For if we begin with a subject, especially if that subject is man, it is easy to treat everything outside the subject, that is, the whole world of objects, in a purely subjective way and to deal with them only as they enter the consciousness of a subject and establish themselves and dwell in that consciousness. It is best to state plainly *that every subject also exists as an object, an objective "something" or "somebody."*

"As an object, a man is 'somebody'—and this sets him apart from every other entity in the visible world, which as an object is always only 'something'."[123] I quote this passage from Karol Wojtyla's *Love and Responsibility* because it seems to summarize neatly the results of our study. It gives us a compass to guide our reinterpretation of Aquinas. As Aquinas himself would say, *postremus in executione primus in intentione.* This dictum opens the door to a *rapprochement* between the Thomistic revival and the newer, modern context within which this revival is occurring.

Consider a few of Wojtyla's main affirmations: "The world in which we live is made up of a great number of objects."[124] This statement is easily connected to the opening passage of Ludwig Wittgenstein's *Tractatus Logico-Philosophicus.* For Wittgenstein, as for Wotjyla, the world is composed of facts: The starting point is objectivism and the world as given by sensible experience. Above all, the object is that which presents itself as an object of sense experience. If we supplement the first affirmation with the more precise one that immediately follows, then the "object" is synonymous with "being," clearly echoing the Thomistic-Aristotelian idea that *ens* (that which appears to experience and is furnished with the qualities of being) is the starting point for philosophy. The Thomistic notion of *ens* is a complete transformation of Wittgenstein's objectivist starting point since a "fact" is something quite different from the object understood as *ens.*

A fact is a particular unified perception of the world. The object, however, is a concretized articulation of being endowed with the possibility of

123 Karol Wojtyła, *Love and Responsibility* (San Francisco: Ignatius Press, 1993), p. 21
124 *Ibid.*

being perceived in the world. That is to say that the object presupposes the presence or attribution of a real substrate to which the perception adheres. Indeed, the very notion of object presupposes the existence of two real substrates that the objective side and the subjective side of perception adhere to, respectively. The perceptive unity is therefore explicitly tied to a real object that causes the perception. More proximately, the perceptive unity is tied to a particular "subject" that is now the subject of the perception. The object is in fact that which stands in front of (*Gegenstand* in German) a subject. This articulation of subject and object challenges Wittgenstein's notion of the impersonality of the event.

This subjective-personal character of knowledge implicit in the notion of object and obtained dialectically is rendered more evident through the notion of *ens*. Indeed, *ens* can be further qualified as an object or a subject. The subject, insofar as it exists, has a substantial existence and a *hypokeimenon* and is therefore an object. More precisely, it is an object with the quality of being a subject. There is no such thing as "pure subjectivity" amounting to a pure *intelligere* or a pure *percepire*. Understanding and perceiving always adhere to an individual substance that exercises the acts of understanding and perceiving. That is to say that understanding and perceiving are acts of a person. At this point, Wojtyla has prepared all the elements that will serve to enrich, so to speak, the Thomistic perspective, without losing the solidity of the essential ontological foundation of the person.

Wojtyla makes it clear from the beginning that if "object" is used synonymously with *ens,* then "this is not the proper meaning of the word, since an 'object,' strictly speaking, is something related to a 'subject'. A 'subject' is also an 'entity'—an entity which exists and acts in a certain way."[125] As we have already seen, the notion of *ens* is wider than "object." Objects are a category of *entes*. Alongside them, within the genus *ens,* are subjects. So the subject is also, in a broad sense, an object *(ens)* insofar as it is endowed with a real substrate. It is here, after these more precise clarifications are made, that the objectivist starting point is completely overturned: "It is then possible to say that the world in which we live is composed of many subjects. It would indeed be proper to speak of 'subjects' before 'objects.'"[126]

125 *Ibid.*
126 *Ibid.*

This claim needs further explanation. It draws attention to the fact that, in order for us to understand the world and our relation to it, it is more important for us to understand the phenomenon of the person than the laws that govern objective phenomena. The experience of objective reality must be soaked in by the person and used for its own *nature* so that it can complete its own growth and maturation. The human world is, therefore, above all, a world inhabited by persons and only secondarily a place of things. This accords with what psychology, sociology, and psychoanalysis tell us: From the very beginning of life, personal relationships have a decisive impact on the possibility of man's material life, both with regard to the development of his affective maturity and his future happiness or unhappiness. This also accords with the *a priori* foundation of modern philosophy. Modern philosophy substantially distinguishes itself in this regard, for modern philosophy does not begin with *ens* but with man—that is, with the subject.

This turns the objectivist approach on its head. But does that mean it is some kind of a card trick, akin to the slight-of-hand contemporary theology uses to free itself from tradition while seeming to remain faithful to it? Why do we start with the object if, at least from one point of view, it would be more correct to say the world is a collection of subjects?

"If the order has been reversed here," explains Wojtyla, "the intention was to put the emphasis right at the beginning of this book on its objectivism, its realism. For if we begin with a 'subject,' especially when that subject is man, it is easy to treat everything which is outside the subject, i.e. the whole world of objects, in a purely subjective way, to deal with it only as it enters into the consciousness of a subject, establishes itself and dwells in that consciousness."[127] We can express this in another way: We cannot simply start with the subject because it has already become the starting point for modern philosophy, and because modern philosophy has used it incorrectly and obscured it.

But does this mean that we should avoid beginning with subject? Not at all. It means we should follow it with particular methodological caution so that a correct emphasis on the unique importance of the real subject does not lead us to a modern hypostatization of abstract subjectivity. If we

127 *Ibid.*

want to value the real human subject, we must never forget that it is also an object and that it therefore exists with an objective structure of subjectivity. Hence it is on the basis of the objective structure of subjectivity—implicitly contained in Aquinas—that we can sensibly attempt to recover subjectivity.

This can be described methodologically in several different ways. We could say that it develops the modern theme of subjectivity within the philosophy of existence without contradicting it. We could also say that it involves not so much reconciliation between the philosophy of being and the modern philosophy of subjective conscience as bringing to mature synthesis the two great currents of Christian thought: the Augustinian-Anselmian and the Thomistic. We might also say that, within Thomistic thought, it involves the development of a more complete anthropology by inserting into the objective consideration of the human person those subjective aspects of personal relation that Aquinas develops in his teaching on angelic substances and the Trinity, taking care, of course, not to confuse these two levels of personal existence.

Each of these respective definitions contains an element of truth. Taken together, they define a program of philosophical research that in a certain sense goes beyond Aquinas in the direction of modern philosophy, but toward modern philosophy on a road indicated by Aquinas as an alternative to the Avicennian-Averroistic road. It is a "modernity" as much aware of "becoming" as it is of "*that which* becomes." Consequently, it is aware of the substantial *unity of philosophy* that runs contrary to the modern mindset, even though it is only by retrieving this substantial philosophical unity that we can address the fundamental questions of reality: i.e., what is the human subject, and what is the relationship between human subjects in a permanent, ontic, metaphysical structure?